T0273250

High-Tech Protectionism

The Irrationality of Antidumping Laws

Claude Barfield

The AEI Press

Publisher for the American Enterprise Institute

WASHINGTON, D.C.

2003

For all other inquiries please contact the AEI Press, 1150 Seventeenth Street, N.W., Washington, D.C. 20036 or call 1-800-862-5801.

Library of Congress Cataloging-in-Publication Data

Barfield, Claude E.
    High-tech protectionism : the irrationality of antidumping laws /
Claude Barfield.
        p. cm.
    Includes bibliographical references.
    ISBN 0-8447-7168-6 (paper)
    1. Antidumping duties—Law and legislation. 2. Dumping
(International trade)—Law and legislation. 3. High technology
industries—Law and legislation. 4. Supercomputer industry—Law
and legislation. 5. Semiconductor industry—Law and legislation.
6. Steel industry and trade—Law and legislation. I. Title.

K4635.B365 2003
343'.08745004—dc22

                                                                2003055766

1 3 5 7 9 10 8 6 4 2

Table of Contents

FIGURES

TABLES

Acknowledgments

The author would like to thank Cordula Thum, Andrei Zlate, and Frank Fu for research assistance and some initial drafting for sections of this study. In addition, he is grateful for the comments and critiques offered by Michael Finger, James Durling, Gary Horlick, Douglas Irwin, and Patrick Messerlin, who read portions or all of preliminary drafts of the manuscript.

1

Introduction

The explosion of high-technology products onto the world market, in addition to making many aspects of our lives easier, is one of the principal engines driving economic growth.[1] In computers, pharmaceuticals, telecommunications, the Internet, and countless other areas, advances in high-technology sectors are redefining the way we live. High-technology sectors cover a range of industries, of course, but they share one defining trait—they require intensive research and development (R&D) for inputs, either directly at the final manufacturing stage or through the intermediate goods used in their production. The capital outlays, while varying by industry, are often quite large and well beyond the capacity of single individuals or firms.

In an era of globalization, it should not come as a surprise that the competitive environment is much more intense. Contrary to what some misguided politicians and antiglobal activists have argued, however, foreign competition has served both American companies and consumers well. In addition to introducing a range of new products to consumers, competition (both domestic and foreign) is forcing most U.S. companies to become more efficient.

A prerequisite for reaping the benefits of foreign competition, of course, is an international trading system that fosters the free flow of goods, services, and investment among nations. Broadly speaking, such a system exists. From the signing of the General Agreement on Tariffs and Trade (GATT) in 1947, to the formation in 1995 of its successor, the World Trade Organization (WTO), the multilateral trading system has become increasingly open, with trade and investment barriers steadily coming down. The result is that global economic welfare has increased, and millions have been lifted out of grinding poverty.

Unfortunately, no institutional system is perfect, and the multilateral trade regime is no exception. WTO rules allow countries to arbitrarily define "unfair" trading practices of other countries and to restrict the free flow of goods by invoking trade remedy laws designed to protect domestic industries. Unable to compete effectively on their merits, companies can ask governments to restrict foreign competition, rather than becoming more efficient. The weapon of choice for many of these companies is antidumping law. The law targets allegedly "unfair" trading practices of foreign competitors accused of exporting (or "dumping") products into a foreign market at prices below the cost of production, or below the prices charged in domestic or third markets (price discrimination). If a foreign competitor is found guilty of dumping, the WTO Antidumping Agreement of 1994 allows countries to impose antidumping duties on those imports (Boltuck and Litan 1991; Lindsey 1999).

Antidumping laws are fundamentally at odds with the free trade policies that have dramatically increased global economic welfare over the past half-century. They are tantamount to "WTO-legalized protectionism" and a "major loophole in the free-trade disciplines of the world trading system," in the words of Brink Lindsey of the Cato Institute (Lindsey 1999, 5). Further, the procedures by which antidumping laws are applied are arbitrary and do not properly identify allegedly "unfair" trading practices. Antidumping laws also do little to offer effective remedies for companies that claim to have been "materially injured" by "unfair" foreign competitors and their pricing practices.

Two facts about the recent history of antidumping actions should be underscored: First, there has been a great proliferation in the use of antidumping cases among WTO members (particularly by developing countries), combined with a rising number of cases targeting the United States. Second, the current Doha Round of WTO negotiations is being jeopardized by a backlash against the antidumping rules and by threats to block trade liberalization in other areas unless the antidumping rules are reformed.

Figure 1 shows the trend in new antidumping measures for both developed and developing countries from 1979 to 2002. For the past decade (1990–2002), developed country new antidumping measures have fluctuated from a low of 33 to a high of 105. But the striking change has come in the numbers for developing countries, which have risen almost steadily each year from 3 in 1990 to a high of 146 in 2002. By mid-2002, India (150 measures in place), South Africa (98), Mexico (61), and Argentina (58) were moving up the ranks to join the United States (264), the European Union (219), Canada (90), and Australia (56) as the most frequent antidumping users (WTO 2002a). Both developed and developing countries have been targeting more users. At the end of 2002,

FIGURE 1
ANTIDUMPING MEASURES BY IMPORTING COUNTRIES:
DEVELOPING VS. DEVELOPED COUNTRIES, 1979–2002

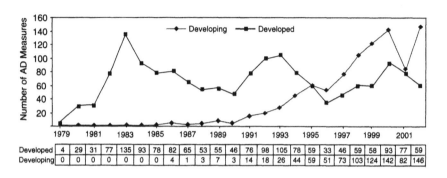

	1979		1981		1983		1985		1987		1989		1991		1993		1995		1997		1999		2001	
Developed	4	29	31	77	135	93	78	82	65	53	55	46	76	98	105	78	59	33	46	59	58	93	77	59
Developing	0	0	0	0	0	0	0	4	1	3	7	3	14	18	26	44	59	51	73	103	124	142	82	146

Source: WTO 2002a.
Note: All of the high-income OECD members (23 countries in total) are counted as "developing" countries.

the United States led the brigade, with actions in place against 48 countries; but developing countries were also expanding their antidumping targets: between 1995 and 2002, India jumped from 7 to 39 countries; Brazil from 12 to 24; and Mexico from 13 to 17 targeted countries. The European Union maintained measures in place against 34 countries at the end of 2002 (WTO 2003a).

And finally, the United States stood third behind China and South Korea as the most popular target of antidumping investigations. From January 1995 through December 2002, the United States was the subject of 115 investigations initiated by 18 different countries. During the same time interval, 67 definitive measures were imposed against U.S. exports (WTO 2003f).

Antidumping: A Threat to Future WTO Negotiations

Though developing countries, defensively, have become keen students of the protectionist antidumping game, they are still novices, far behind the United States and the European Union in the exploitation of antidumping actions to stifle international competition. The United States, with over 250 measures in place, and the EU, with more than 200, still far outdistanced even the most eager learners among the developing countries.

It should come as no surprise, then, that reform of the WTO antidumping rules has become a hotly debated topic in the new Doha Round of multilateral trade negotiations. Leading developing countries such as Brazil, Korea, China, Mexico, Argentina, Egypt, South Africa, and others have threatened to hold all other negotiating issues hostage to changes in this protectionist vestige from the past. Japan has also been a leading advocate of reform as a result of its long history as the chief target of antidumping actions by the United States and European countries (*International Trade Reporter* [*ITR*] November 1, 2001; May 2, 2002).

Demands for fundamental changes in WTO trade remedy rules will present the Bush administration with its most difficult challenge in the Doha Round negotiations. In the run-up to the launching of the round in November 2001, while the administration beat back attempts in Congress to tie its hands completely, both houses of Congress passed strongly worded resolutions advising the president not to agree to major revisions in the current regime. The House of Representatives resolution passed 410 to 4 just one week before the Doha meeting (*ITR* November 15, 2001). Defenders of U.S. trade laws wanted the administration to veto *any* discussion of these issues in the upcoming negotiations.

In order to break a deadlock that would have prevented the launch of the new round, however, U.S. Trade Representative Robert Zoellick agreed to language that placed trade remedies laws on the table—but, at least in the American view, under tightly restricted conditions and terms. The Doha Declaration allows negotiations "aimed at clarifying and improving disciplines" under the WTO's existing antidumping and subsidies agreements, but the mandate also states that such negotiations will preserve the "basic concepts, principles and effectiveness of these Agreements, their objectives and instruments" (*ITR* November 15, 2001; February 14, 2002).

In preliminary negotiations since November 2001, proponents of major reform in the existing WTO trade remedy regimes have put forward increasingly bold proposals for technical reforms of current antidumping rules, calculations, and procedures. The United States has firmly resisted all of these proposals, arguing that they violate the Doha Declaration's mandate that negotiations preserve the "basic concepts, principles, and effectiveness" of existing antidumping national regimes (*ITR* May 2, 2002; May 9, 2002; July 7, 2002; October 17, 2002; October 24, 2002).

Clearly, the Bush administration's strategy is to wait until the very end of the Doha Round negotiations before dealing with proposed antidumping reforms. What defenders of the current system fear—and opponents hope for—is that in order to seal a "grand bargain" in the closing hours of negotiations, U.S. Trade Representative Zoellick will be forced (or will claim to be forced) to accept at least some of the major demands that have been put forward by developing countries. The problem with this approach is that developing countries thus far have been adamant in opposing any interim agreements absent movement on antidumping issues. Thus, the outcome of antidumping negotiations—and of the Doha Round itself—remains doubtful.[2]

The Folly of Antidumping Actions in High-Tech Sectors

While the application of antidumping laws is problematic in any sector, it is particularly troublesome in high-technology sectors for three primary reasons. First, given the inherently dynamic nature of high-technology sectors, the specific products which have duties imposed upon them are often obsolete by the time the inevitably contentious antidumping case is resolved. The famous Moore's Law (Gordon Moore was a cofounder and later chairman of Intel) that capacity of semiconductor chips doubles every eighteen months still holds. Under such conditions, the petitioner in the domestic market rarely achieves meaningful relief. Second, identifying so-called strategic industries is usually a fool's errand; in many cases what is labeled "strategic" in one year quickly becomes merely a commodity over the next few years (for example, dynamic random access memory [DRAM] semiconductors). Third, the high degree of multisourcing from different countries in the chain of production results in situations where antidumping duties are sometimes actually imposed on domestic competitors (Hindley and Messerlin 1996).

Over the past two decades, the United States has compiled a dismal record in its attempts to use antidumping actions as an industrial policy tool to create, foster, or protect important high-tech sectors. The goal of this study is to set forth the history of these actions for policymakers and the interested public in a nontechnical manner, and to draw public policy conclusions and recommendations from this analysis. Specifically, the study will analyze how American antidumping laws have been applied in three high-technology industries: supercomputers, flat-panel displays (FPDs), and DRAM computer chips. In addition, the study will examine the U.S. steel industry. Today, steel is considered the quintessential "basic" industry, one which naturally gravitated to less developed economies that enjoy a comparative advantage from the abundance of cheap, unskilled labor and production techniques that prize brawn over brains. This study's conclusions regarding steel, however, are twofold: First, traditional industries such as steel can survive in advanced industrial economies if they become "high-tech" industries by moving rapidly up the technological ladder through the introduction of advanced industrial processes and techniques. Second, government intervention to protect increasingly obsolete domestic steel technologies, symbolized by Big Steel (the integrated U.S. steel companies), has only hindered the emergence of a truly competitive, technologically advanced steel sector, symbolized (and actualized) by the so-called minimills (which use advanced technologies to transform scrap steel into semifinished and finished products).

The most important policy conclusion of this analysis is that protectionist antidumping actions had the following general results: (1) negative consequences for other industries, U.S. consumers, and workers that far outweighed the purported protectionist benefits (DRAMs, FPDs, and steel); (2) political interventions that traduced the integrity of administrative and legal processes (supercomputers and FPDs); (3) dumping actions that were based upon the historically erroneous prediction that U.S. competitiveness was inextricably wrapped up in the protection of a particular "strategic" industry (DRAMs, supercomputers, FPDs, and steel); and (4) the serendipitous appearance of new technologies that rendered irrelevant the original antidumping actions (DRAMs and supercomputers).

Regarding individual industries, antidumping actions had the following results: Antidumping actions in DRAMs transferred at least $4–5 billion dollars from U.S. computer manufacturers and consumers to Japanese semiconductor companies. Antidumping actions on flat-panel displays ultimately drove U.S. and foreign computer manufacturers offshore, displacing thousands of American workers. Despite the predictions of handwringing industrial policy advocates, the U.S. economy has not only survived but thrived without an FPD industry. The naked political intervention of the Commerce Department in the supercomputer case resembled the actions of a third world government. Finally, in the case of the longest and most costly government intervention—steel—the cost to American taxpayers has been estimated at between $46 billion and $74 billion.

2

Trends in High-Technology Trade

Competition: The Key to Innovation

Two factors have played a pivotal role in fostering the growth of high-technology industries. The first is an education system that nurtures creative individuals and allows them the freedom to innovate. The second factor, competition and the ability to reap rewards from success, is less readily apparent. While individual inventors may be willing to take years to bring a product to market, the investors who are so critical to providing the necessary capital for R&D are not. And while inventors may in some cases have such a passionate devotion to their profession that they are less interested in and willing to eschew financial remuneration, the investors who provide the capital to fund advances are guided primarily by profit motive.

Competition has spurred innovation. This is particularly so in high-technology sectors because the product life of many new technologies is short. A defining characteristic of high-technology sectors is that in some form or other they seem to be subject to "Moore's Law," which as noted above states that the amount of performance received per dollar spent doubles every eighteen months because of technical innovation. Computers built three years ago are now largely obsolete. Older computer chips are now almost worthless as improvements in the techniques of electronic data storage allow businesses and consumers to store ever-increasing amounts of data on ever-smaller microchips. Or think of a company that relied solely on selling, for example, hand-held calculators (which cost, on average, one hundred dollars in 1972). If that company did not invest in R&D to expand the range of functions the calculator could perform, it would be out of business. In the year 2002, there are hand-held units that, in addition to performing the functions of a calculator, serve as your appointment and address book, allow you to send and receive electronic mail, and store large amounts of data. In short, one must constantly innovate or be swept aside.

7

The Globalization of High-Technology Trade

In the 1950s and 1960s, the United States clearly enjoyed a comparative advantage in many high-technology sectors, and the American economy was the envy of the world—so much so that foreign businessmen at the time were fearful that by 1980 the Americans would have a monopoly on science, knowledge, and power. That did not happen. In the 1970s and 1980s, many European and East Asian companies' R&D expenditures began outpacing their American competitors. Not surprisingly, both regions developed a range of new, innovative products.

While many variables influence productivity growth, it is clear that lower investments in R&D are strongly correlated with lower productivity growth rates. In the 1950s and 1960s, when American R&D expenditures were growing at 6 percent per year, productivity growth for the private sector averaged around 2.75 percent annually. In the 1970s and 1980s, when U.S. investment in R&D first declined and then registered only small real annual gains, productivity for the private sector averaged around 1.2 percent annually (Scherer 1992; Boskin and Lau 1996). A direct consequence of this economic malaise was the palpable fear that the United States was losing its competitive edge. Some even went so far as to say, "The Cold War is over and Japan won" (Johnson 1995). Others predicted that the U.S. economy would be "hollowed out" and that Americans would trade "low value" goods for "higher value" goods made overseas.

In the first decade of the twenty-first century, it is clear that the above prediction was far off the mark. In the late 1990s, total R&D spending in the United States grew at an annual rate of just under 6 percent, while productivity averaged 2.6 percent growth between 1995 and 2001. In high-tech sectors from biotechnology to high-end electronics (computer systems, software, telecommunications), U.S. industries far outdistanced world competitors. The January 2001 Economic Report of the President described the combination of factors that produced these beneficent economic results:

> Why, then is the U.S. economy awash in technology? The evidence suggests that the combination of increased competition-driven demand for technology, thriving financial markets, increased public and private R&D, and legal protection have created a uniquely favorable climate for entrepreneurship in the technology sector. . . . It is not any one of these factors in isolation but rather the convergence of the favorable conditions that has led to the recent surge in technological innovation. Technology flourishes

when markets are allowed to work, and where government policy provides essential support. (Council of Economic Advisors 2001, 119–120)

It should be noted, finally, that even with the bursting of the "dot.com" bubble in 2001, U.S. productivity growth has remained above 3 percent, and the United States remains at the top competitively in the sectors it came to dominate in the 1990s (Council of Economic Advisors 2003). Capital goods, which are composed largely of high-technology goods, still constitute over 40 percent of U.S. exports.

To be sure, the specific response of U.S. companies to the challenge of increased foreign competition varies by both industry and individual firms. In a variety of ways, though, firms are interacting and seizing opportunities that the increasingly global economy offers. Whether through joint ventures, wholly owned subsidiaries, or even establishment of plants overseas to produce a product (or part of a product), a number of companies are reaping the benefits of globalization.

High-tech companies in particular are becoming increasingly global. For many such companies, there is an emerging international division of labor, in which countries can specialize in the manufacture of individual components for complex products, rather than the entire product. Some companies, for example, have set up research facilities overseas with impressive results. Swiss and German scientists based in Switzerland but working for IBM, for example, made key breakthroughs on high-temperature superconductivity. Similarly, Texas Instruments' software has engineering laboratories in India, while Toyota has a major research center in southern California.

The specifics of the four industries surveyed here—supercomputers, flat panels, DRAMs, and steel—are discussed below. The broader point, though, is that increased foreign competition has greatly benefited the companies that have risen to the challenge. To be sure, companies have to work harder, be more savvy, and break new technological frontiers, but the payoff is quite large. In the words of one of the world's leading economists, Frederick M. Scherer:

> As more and more nations have elected to play the trading game according to the new high-technology rules, participants have had to run twice as fast in order to secure the rewards of leadership—substantial export and foreign subsidiary sales, supra-normal profit margins, and for employees, compensation providing the purchasing power to enjoy a high and improving standard of living. (Scherer 1992, 173)

3

Antidumping Laws: The Easy Way to Stay in the Market

Some companies have failed to seize the new opportunities that global-ization offers. Finding themselves unable to compete, they turn to gov-ernment for assistance. Over the course of the past few decades, the means by which these companies can procure government assistance have dwindled. Tariffs and quotas are largely disappearing, and direct subsidies and bailouts, while they still occur, do so much less frequently. Unfortunately, there remain two important outlets for companies to restrict imports and foreign competition. Both deal with import surges. One is the special safeguard law, which will be discussed further later; the other is the antidumping law.

The specific failing of the U.S. antidumping law in the four sectors is discussed below. At the outset, though, a broader look at some of the problems with the law is warranted. While this discussion is limited to U.S. law, it applies to the antidumping laws of many other countries as well. (For detailed references to the material in this section, see Lawrence [ed.] 1998; Hindley and Messerlin 1996; Litan and Boltuck 1991.)

Economists identify a number of different categories of "dumping" actions, related to the underlying motivations of the exporting company (Willig 1998). Market-expansion dumping takes place when there are differences in demand between two discrete and separable markets. Cyclical dumping occurs when a sudden downturn in demands creates a situation of oversupply. State-trading dumping occurs when a non-market economy wants to get hard currency or creates an oversupply in an industry due to poor planning. None of these types of dumping is meant to create monopoly conditions. Under most circumstances, econ-omists believe these are relatively benign forms of dumping, unless accompanied by other private market or government practices.

The actions that should most concern proponents of antidumping laws occur when companies engage in dumping in order to increase market power to such a high degree that they will be able to charge monopoly prices later. Broadly speaking, economists identify two categories of actions that could constitute anticompetitive dumping onto a market.

The first type of market-power dumping is known as "predatory dumping." This occurs when companies export at low prices to drive rivals out of business and obtain monopoly power. Four basic prerequisites are necessary for predatory dumping to take place successfully. First, a country must possess a large market share at home that is protected or serves as a "sanctuary market." Second, there must be an opportunity to invade another market to obtain larger market shares. Third, if there are several producers in the domestic market, they must collude in order to maintain the long-term price hike that is possible after the foreign market firms have been driven out of business. Finally, significant barriers to entry must exist in the industry. If not, the price hike would create strong incentives for competitors to enter the market and undermine the monopolistic position (Willig 1998).

The second form of dumping relates to the expansion of market power and is referred to as "strategic dumping." Strategic dumping combines low export prices with a protected home market to give exporters an advantage in industries with static (fixed R&D and capital expenses) or dynamic (learning by doing) economies of scale. With access to both home and foreign markets, foreign firms gain a cost advantage over domestic firms that are unable to compete abroad. This advantage allegedly eventually gives the exporting firms market power (Hindley and Messerlin 1996).

Assigning motivations to a particular firm's reasons for dumping is difficult at best. Antidumping laws do not require a country to investigate behavior that is consistent or inconsistent with normal competition. All that petitioners must show is that dumping and "unfair" pricing is taking place and that they have been "materially injured" somehow. A brief review of the process illustrates these flaws.

Dumping cases are handled by two U.S. government agencies. The Department of Commerce establishes whether or not dumping is taking place and to what degree. This process is essentially pro forma: Between 1980 and 1997, the department ruled that dumping was taking place in 96 percent of the cases it reviewed (804 of 837 petitions). The case then proceeds to the U.S. International Trade Commission (USITC), which decides whether the U.S. industry in question is suffering injury. If the USITC finds injury is occurring, the dumping companies are required to place a cash deposit or bond with U.S. Customs equal to the dumping margin deter-mined by the Commerce Department. Provisions are in place to review these findings, and vary by circumstance.

The methodologies, though, upon which these two agencies rely are arbitrary at best and based on faulty methodologies at worst (Ikenson 2001; Lindsey and Ikenson 2002a). First, comparing prices between markets is difficult. In addition to variations on the demand side due to consumer preferences, on the supply side there is tremendous variation in costs of different factors of production, whether it is the cost of inputs or the cost of labor. All of these factors exert great influence on the price of a product in a given market.

Second, there are considerable asymmetries in the methodology used to calculate price differences between markets. Economists have long established that under typical competitive conditions, firms will sell products at marginal, not average, costs. The U.S. antidumping law equates fair value with average costs plus an allowance for profit. It is thus possible for a firm to be selling at exactly the same price as the U.S. firm and be found guilty of dumping.

Third, even if one accepts the methodology used by U.S. government agencies, it is difficult to discern whether or not dumping is taking place at all since the law does not require evidence of the one variable that tran-scends all forms of market-expanding dumping—a "sanctuary" or pro-tected home market. It seems reasonable to conclude that if dumping can only take place in the context of governments abroad enacting regula-tions to protect their home market, then these practices should at least be investigated (Hindley and Messerlin 1996).

The failings of the U.S. antidumping law are vividly evident in the four case histories that we turn to now: supercomputers, flat-panel displays, DRAM computer chips, and steel.

4

The Supercomputer Story

Background

In the spring of 1996, the University Corporation for Atmospheric Research (UCAR), an agency funded by the National Science Foundation (NSF), signaled its intention to award a $32.25 million contract for a supercomputer system to NEC, a Japanese company. When UCAR's intention became known, Cray, the leading U.S. supercomputer manufacturer, immediately went into action—first lobbying Congress to prevent the award and ultimately filing an antidumping petition with the Commerce Department alleging that NEC was dumping in order to force American manufacturers out of the market (Maur and Messerlin 1999).

Even before the formal petition, two highly significant political events occurred. First, Congressman David Obey (D-WI), who represented Cray, introduced an amendment, which the House of Representatives passed, that would have withheld the salaries of NSF personnel if they awarded the contract to the Japanese company. At the same time, on their own, political officials at the Commerce Department launched an investigation that concluded—to no one's surprise—that dumping existed. An assistant secretary of commerce also informed the NSF that the NEC sale would "threaten the U.S. supercomputer industry with material injury"—a determination that only the USITC is supposed to make after a careful analysis of market conditions (Goldman 1996; Maggs 1996, 1997; *Inside U.S. Trade* May 24, 1996; Dumler 1997).

Despite the charged political atmosphere, NSF officials pushed ahead with plans to award the contract to NEC. They did so for two reasons: First, NSF's trade consultant concluded (contrary to Commerce's finding) that dumping had not occurred. Second, NSF officials steadfastly believed NEC had submitted a much superior bid. They reaffirmed this belief (despite congressional threats to their salaries) throughout the proceedings that followed. Indeed, much later in the USITC final hearings, the director of the competitive bid process stated that the Cray machine met only one of four technical criteria of the contract. For that reason, UCAR concluded that NEC "offered and demonstrated overwhelmingly superior technical performance and low risk relative to Cray" (*Inside U.S. Trade* August 2, 1996).

Subsequently, the Commerce Department found a dumping margin of 454 percent, and the USITC followed with a determination of "material injury." Interestingly, unlike other Japanese companies in other proceedings, NEC throughout the process took bold and defiant stances—actually to the discomfort and dismay of the Ministry of International Trade and Industry, which feared American retaliation on other trade and diplomatic issues. NEC refused to cooperate with the Commerce Department during the proceedings and publicly stated that Cray had not—and could not—meet the bid requirements. It directly challenged the handling of the case, and appealed the department's and the USITC's final determinations to the Court of International Trade and then to a federal circuit court, arguing in part that political intervention had corrupted the decision-making process. Ultimately, NEC lost the appeals, and the antidumping duties went into effect (U.S. International Trade Commission 1999b).

The supercomputer proceedings teach a remarkable series of lessons, some of which duplicate lessons from the experience in semiconductors and advanced flat-panel displays. With supercomputers, as with semiconductors and flat panels, government officials either never understood or willfully ignored the structure of the industry and the nature of worldwide competition in the sector. With supercomputers, as with semiconductors and flat panels, they seemed blissfully unaware of technological trajectories in the industry. Knowledge of industry structure and competition, as well as future technological pathways, demonstrate how unlikely (if not impossible) it is for predatory tactics—the only real justification for antidumping actions—to succeed in this industry.

The Structure of the Supercomputer Industry and the Nature of Competition

Industrial policy proponents, who argue that antidumping is a key tool for "leveling the playing field" and allowing U.S. firms to keep up with foreign (particularly Asian) competitors, have identified supercomputers (and specifically Cray, as the leading American company in the area) as strategic assets that must be protected at all costs. With supercomputers and other high-tech electronic sectors, they despaired of matching the *keiretsu* system (a system of close ties among producers and suppliers) of Japanese companies, which benefit from strong financial ties and low costs of capital. As industrial policy advocate Maria Anchordoguy has lamented, Japanese "corporate structure seems to be more suitable to the development of high-cost, high-risk technologies such as supercomputers" (Anchordoguy 1994, 39).

Yet the record of recent years belies these gloom and doom forecasts, even as it raises doubts about the use of antidumping as an industrial policy tool for the United States. A look at the evolving structure of the supercomputer industry and who is competing with whom in that market illustrates why this is so.

Supercomputers are often divided into three main categories based on processor architecture (the key input of the machines): vector processors and parallel vector processors (PVPs), massively parallel processors (MPPs) and symmetric multiprocessor systems (SMPs).[3] The Cray and NEC computers that formed the basis of the antidumping action were both vector computers; significantly, the USITC confined the affected market for calculating antidumping margins narrowly to vector computers.

Processors used in supercomputers can be divided into two categories: "off-the-shelf" processors and custom processors. Custom processors are used in PVPs; they are very powerful chips designed for a specific architecture. "Off-the-shelf" processors are basically commodity chips, and are used in MPPs and SMPs. Large semiconductor manufacturers make them for use in both supercomputers and for less advanced mainframes and servers. Supercomputers made with them are substantially cheaper than those with custom chips, but until recently they lacked the flexibility and capability of custom processors. That situation is changing rapidly and will form a key part of our story.

Changes in technology and resulting shifts in market structure, with the entrance of new players, highlight the general absurdity of U.S. antidumping analysis and the inability of government officials to fathom not only trends in the distant future but also short-term trends right under their noses. A recent study by Jean-Christophe Maur and Patrick Messerlin has calculated changes in the markets for various supercomputer technologies, as well as the growth of computing power. They trace the steeply rising total capacity of supercomputers in the mid-1990s, with huge increases between 1995 and 1997 (the period of the antidumping investigation) resulting from the introduction of RISC technology for MPPs and a new generation of parallel vector systems. Of greater significance for the Cray/NEC case is the revolution that occurred in the competition between vector and non-vector supercomputers. Astonishingly, the share of the supercomputer market supplied by vector computers dropped from almost 35 percent in 1993 to 1.2 percent in 1999, rendering the competitive struggle between Cray and NEC vector computers virtually irrelevant to true market trajectories (Maur and Messerlin 1999).

Further, because of technological leaps, particularly with regard to MPPs, the global supercomputer industry experienced major structural changes. First, new companies entered the market, most of which were large established electronic or computer firms such as IBM, Hewlett-Packard, Intel, and Sun Microsystems. The reason for their sudden appearance was that their position in "off-the-shelf" processors allowed them to gain a footing in the supercomputer market. In addition, because of the squeeze from new competition, the industry concentrated, with Cray being absorbed by SGI, Convex by Hewlett-Packard, and Digital by Compaq. Today, they share the bulk of the world market with Cray (SGI), the historic industry leader (U.S. National Science and Technology Council 1999; Maur and Messerlin 1999).

Finally, there is Cray's charge that NEC's UCAR bid was part of a pattern of Japanese predatory dumping. In a press release, SGI stated: "Japanese vendors of supercomputers are attempting to drive U.S. competition from the market by establishing unsustainable low prices for such systems" (Maur and Messerlin 1999, 7). (This is close to the textbook definition of predation—that is, decrease prices in order to drive competition out of business and introduce even larger monopoly prices afterward.) What is the likelihood that NEC could have pulled off this feat? First, let us examine the entire supercomputer market and then narrow the focus to vector supercomputers.

In assessing the potential for successful predation, there are several tests that can be introduced: Is there the possibility of large market power in the U.S. market? Is there the possibility of large market power in the world market? Is there collusion among Japanese firms? Are there significant barriers to entry into the sector? None of these tests is positive for Japanese supercomputer firms.

First, the Japanese share of the total supercomputer market in the United States ran between 2 and 3 percent during the 1990s. Second, the market share of Japanese supercomputers worldwide was about 15 percent, again an unlikely base from which to embark upon predation.

Regarding the potential collusion among Japanese supercomputer firms, NEC, Hitachi, and Fujitsu are about the same size in terms of capacity installed, and industry specialists cite evidence that they compete vigorously in foreign markets. At the same time, Hitachi has turned away from vector supercomputers entirely, while Fujitsu and NEC generally pursue different end-use capabilities. Finally, given the sizable numbers of new entrants into the supercomputer fields, clearly barriers to entry are not high or offputting (U.S. International Trade Commission 1999).

There is, however, one ironic potential result of the antidumping assault on Japanese companies. With Japanese market share stagnant or falling in America (and around the world), and with the industry consolidation that is proceeding apace in the United States, a growing risk of anticompetitive behavior by U.S. firms is not impossible. In other words, the antidumping system essentially protects U.S. supercomputer manufacturers from all foreign competition.

5

Flat-Panel Displays

Background

From the late 1980s, the U.S. government attempted to create an entire industry—flat-panel displays (FPDs)—through industrial policy tools: first, through manipulating the antidumping laws and then through direct subsidy. As with other technologies described in this study, the lessons from this experience are abundant, including the failure of antidumping regimes to distinguish the national interest from private interests; the misuse of antidumping laws to undercut a highly successful industry in computers in favor of a *potential* flat-panel industry; the more or less open collusion between government agencies and private companies in manipulating dumping actions; the ability of the antidumping actions to cause a loss of jobs by forcing companies to move abroad; and finally, the basic flaws in targeting "strategic" industries in the name of industrial policy. The point is the United States during the 1990s never developed a flat-panel industry, and yet it outdistanced all of its major competitors technologically, including the much-feared Japanese, during the same decade (Barfield 1995).

The Flat-Panel-Display Industry

Flat-panel displays are a class of advanced display technologies that have emerged to replace traditional cathode ray tubes because of advantages in weight, small power needs, high resolution, and high information content potential. There are several technologies competing for market share, and a number of niche applications. During the 1980s, pushed by leading Japanese companies, liquid crystal displays (LCDs) became the dominant commercial display technology. LCDs in turn come in two types: active and passive matrix LCDs. The more advanced (active) AMLCDs, which consist of a transistor attached to each pixel (short for picture elements that together form an image on a television screen), figured most prominently in the antidumping actions of the 1990s.

In addition to LCDs, other technologies include plasma display panels (PDPs), in which ionized gases produce the light; field emission displays (FEDs), an improved cathode ray technology that combines with semiconductor technology; and electroluminescent displays (ELDs), which generate light from phosphorus, sandwiched between electrodes. All of these technologies are high-information content (HIC) displays, capable of containing large amounts of information, or pixels. Advanced uses of displays in, for example, high-definition television and computer displays can contain hundreds of thousands of pixels. Not all LCDs are high information; there is still a large market for low-information LCDs in such items as wristwatches, calculators, thermometers, and appliances (Monterey Institute 2001; Hart 1993).

Though U.S. companies pioneered the technology, today Japanese companies control 90 percent of the world market. The reason Japanese companies got in on the ground floor was directly related to their early concentration on low-end consumer electronics. U.S. firms, which pioneered the FPDs, moved out of these markets, and thus were quite willing to license the technologies to Japanese companies, which developed low-information displays for the wristwatches and calculators mentioned above. From this low-tech beginning, Japanese firms moved steadily up the technological ladder to the more advanced LCDs developed in the 1980s.

By the early 1980s, two trends were converging that would dramatically change the market for the FPD industry. First, advances in miniaturization of electronic components and in the computer industry made it realistic to consider manufacturing new products such as laptop computers, handheld televisions, high-definition television, and a new array of advanced information industrial and consumer devices. In addition, corporate planners began to see the outlines of an information revolution in which many human and business activities would be mediated though machine interfaces—even before the revolution that has accompanied the Internet—in the form of sophisticated display (Monterey Institute 2001; Council on Competitiveness 1993).

Japanese FPD companies were extraordinarily well positioned to take advantage of these technological trends. (Although outside the bounds of this paper, it must also be said that in almost all other high-end electronic sectors—particularly those associated with the Internet and allied computer and software applications—the Japanese have fallen steadily behind the United States.) In any case, throughout the 1990s, there were more than a dozen Japanese firms competing in the various LCD technologies. Sharp, Toshiba, Seiko-Epson, Hitachi, Sanyo, and Matsushita were the largest, with Hitachi, Sharp, and a small firm, Hosiden, as clear leaders in AMLCDs. In the United States, in contrast, only one large firm, IBM, had any important presence in this sector, and IBM's effort consisted solely of a joint venture with Toshiba, including a plant in Japan. In the early 1990s, when the antidumping action began, the balance of American LCD manufacturers were very small companies, such as Optical Imaging Systems, Planar, Plasmaco, Photonics Systems, and Electro-Plasma (Hart 1993; Monterey Institute 2001).

The Dumping Petition

It was the U.S. government as much as the private sector that was ultimately responsible for the antidumping petition that was launched against Japanese FPD companies in July 1990. In the late 1980s, concern about the national security implications of Japanese dominance in a number of high-tech electronics sectors, combined with an increasing bureaucratic itch by the Defense Department—particularly its high-tech development arm, the Defense Advanced Research Projects Agency (DARPA)—to take a lead role in restoring U.S. civilian technological leadership, led to pressure from the department for novel mandates. Ironically, while DARPA moved to shore up small U.S. FPD companies, two industry groups, the American Electronics Association and the Computer Systems Policy Project (composed of the leading U.S. computer companies), had turned down requests by U.S. FPD companies for help (Hart 1993; Council on Competitiveness 1993).

In the late 1980s, DARPA convened a number of meetings for small U.S. FPD companies, and in 1990 awarded research contracts to four of them. DARPA also encouraged the companies to form a lobbying arm, the Advanced Display Manufacturing Association (ADMA). And it was DARPA that encouraged the seven companies that formed ADMA to file an antidumping petition against the Japanese companies on July 17, 1990. The petition alleged that Japanese companies intentionally sold FPDs at 10 to 66 percent below cost and thereby had gained 90 percent of the U.S. market. ADMA requested antidumping duties of between 71 and 318 percent as recompense. In a fateful decision, the petition called for duties only on displays and components, not on units assembled outside of the United States. It also directly alleged not only that the Japanese were selling below cost but also that this was a clear case of "predatory pricing" to drive all U.S. firms out of business and attain a complete monopoly (Magee and Yoon 1994; Monterey Institute 2001).

To make a long story short, in September 1990, the USITC issued a preliminary ruling that the U.S. display manufacturers were materially injured. In July 1991, the Commerce Department issued a final determination that AMLCDs and ELDs were being sold below cost and that dumping duties should be imposed. In August 1991, the USITC voted 3–1 to authorize dumping duties of 62.67 percent on AMLCDs and 7.02 percent on ELDs.

The decisions by the Commerce Department and the USITC raise several major issues: How is it that Commerce bent over backwards to define "like product" narrowly in the FPD sector, and then bent over the other way to define "like product" broadly with supercomputers? How does one balance the interest of producers with that of downstream users, the national interest, and the interests of workers in allied industries? Finally, how does one define—and discern—truly "strategic" industries that the United States must retain or create? (Magee and Yoon 1994; Council on Competitiveness 1993).

What's an Industry?

In their original petition, ADMA argued that all four types of FPDs should be treated as one industry. American and Japanese computer companies strongly rebutted this contention, introducing testimony that showed there were substantial differences in physical characteristics, end users, expectations of ultimate purchasers, and distribution channels. They also pointed out that physical properties and characteristics exerted a strong influence on use: for instance, gas plasma is used when picture quality is of great import; and ELDs are best for portable computers and medical and security usage. Both the Commerce Department and the USITC ignored these obvious differences and accepted ADMA's position (Japan Economic Institute 1993; U.S. International Trade Commission 2000).

U.S. computer manufacturers raised a more basic question: Did a display industry even exist in the United States? And, if there were no real industry, how could injury have occurred? IBM, Apple, Compaq, and Tandy filed suit in the Court of International Trade (CIT), claiming that there were no viable U.S. suppliers of AMLCDs—which were essential for desk computers and laptops—and therefore they were dependent on Japanese suppliers. A spokesman for the companies argued that dumping was not involved because "most U.S. [FPD] firms simply are not mass producers of panels for the portable computer market." He also stated that U.S. FPD manufacturers actually "preferred to stay in niche markets such as military products" because then they did not have to face Japanese competition (Monterey Institute 2001).

ADMA introduced—and ultimately the USITC accepted—a wholly novel argument in defending its suit. Implicitly accepting that no real industry existed at the time, it urged the government to agree that forcing Japanese manufacturers to raise their prices to levels that would allow them to compete was the only way they could create an industry through raising capital for R&D and for capital expenditures. The USITC accepted this argument and in its final determination indicated that its decision was intended to encourage U.S. computer manufacturers—at whatever cost—to help build a U.S. industry and stop purchasing from foreign suppliers. In a strange twist of events, in the midst of the proceedings, OIS (the only member of ADMA who made even a small quantity of AMLCDs) filed a request to lift the penalties on these displays, stating that it now agreed that U.S. computers would be hurt by the decision. Later, after further administrative byways, the USITC did finally remove AMLCDs from the penalty box, leaving only the tiny ELDs manufacturers helped by the whole proceeding (Judis 1993; Monterey Institute 2001; Harbrecht, Magnusson, and McWilliams 1993).

The Consequences, Intended and Unintended

While the imposition of antidumping duties did little to help the fledgling and struggling U.S. FPD industry, it did trigger momentous consequences for the computer industry and for some U.S. workers. The imposition of 63 percent duties on imported display screens immediately caused a substantial increase in the price of American-made computers. A spokesman for Compaq estimated that the duty added $1,000 to the cost of building a computer in the United States. Depending on the company, such additional costs—which made them much less competitive with Japanese manufacturers—lasted from months to well over a year, depending on how quickly the company was able to get foreign factories converted or built.

That brings us to a second and even more negative consequence of the action: it impelled both U.S. and Japanese companies to move out of the United States, causing job losses at a number of sites in this country (Johnson 1992). Since the antidumping suit had not included displays that were assembled offshore, the companies moved wholesale. In Compaq's case, it took eighteen months to construct a factory in Scotland, "much against our business plan and against our better judgment," according to a company spokesman (Monterey Institute 2001, 5). Toshiba's American plant in Irvine, California, ceased production of laptops with AMLCDs, while Apple moved production from California to Ireland. Sharp suspended operations in Texas and moved to Canada (Sanger 1991; Monterey Institute 2001). Finally, IBM moved a number of assembly operations offshore to various other locations. As a *Washington Post* writer stated at the time, "The administration's new tariff won't hurt the Japanese. In the fast-growing global market for laptop computers, they will make just as much money shipping display screens somewhere else. The only losers will be American workers who might have had jobs building laptop computers—until the Commerce Department stepped in" (Reid 1991).

Denouement

In the tradition of the Hapsburgs, of whom it has been said that they "forgot nothing and they learned nothing," the Clinton administration in 1994, after the antidumping debacle had ended, launched one further effort to create a U.S.-based FPD industry. (For background and a debate on the material presented in this section, see Barfield 1994, 1995; Flamm 1994, 1995.) This time it hoped to use the cover of national security to subsidize the construction of four plants and achieve a 15 percent slice of the world market in LCDs by the year 2000. With the candor and confidence of a new administration, Clinton White House officials, who conceived the program despite its lodging in Defense, boldly stated that the ultimate purpose was to create a "model for technological development that will equip U.S. companies to break into markets already seized by Japanese companies." First, U.S. companies would compete in the market for LCDs, one White House official stated, and then robotics, ceramics, and precision tools.

With much fanfare, the administration announced plans for a National Flat-Panel Display Initiative that would spend $600 million in seed money to build four LCD plants. Dispassionate critics of the plan, from both the investment and electronics industries as well as from academia, immediately challenged the assumptions behind it. The consensus was that it would take at least $3 billion of public money to come close to capturing 15 percent of the world LCD market. The outlook was bleak, not the least because the Japanese were moving steadily ahead and Korean firms were pouring huge amounts of capital into the same sectors. In addition, defense analysts pointed out, the administration had vastly overestimated defense needs over the next two decades—and existing and planned small niche plants could more than satisfy DOD's requirements (Barfield 1994, 1995). In the end, Congress after 1994 adamantly and wisely refused to fund this grandiose scheme, and the White House and DOD had to settle for small R&D grants and no plants.

For this study, one element of the proposal is of particular significance. The formal planning documents went far beyond technological development and tackled the more difficult tasks of creating and managing a private market, including stimulation of private demand and public procurement. High on the list of actions deemed necessary was the monitoring of world prices in LCDs and trade sanctions and antidumping actions against companies alleged to be engaging in price discrimination or predatory dumping. Thus, along with subsidy inevitably came dumping actions to protect the public investment. The DOD, with this program, had strayed a long way from its national security mission.

Finally, one other longer-term consequence of these attempts to create a new industry through protection or subsidy was predicted, but did not happen. A leading proponent of government intervention to "save" the FPD "industry" warned at the time that losing "generic technologies" like flat-panel screens would make it impossible for the United States to "stay at the technological frontier." ADMA's chief lawyer warned that the U.S. computer industry would rue the day it had not stepped in to help the FPD industry. He warned, "In ten years, we will hear from the computer industry when it is struggling with Japan as we are now." But ten years later, the United States still does not have a flat-panel industry. Yet not only is the U.S. computer industry flourishing, but today the United States also leads the world high-end electronic sectors and from all analyses is pulling steadily ahead of its competitors (Monterey Institute 2001, 5).

6

Semiconductors

A Defining Experience: The U.S.-Japan Crisis of the 1980s

Though an entire decade has passed and the industry and world competitive conditions have changed dramatically, semiconductor trade policy remains haunted by precedents, actions, and mistakes made during the period (1986 to 1991) of extreme conflict between the United States and Japan over semiconductors. From the origin of the industry to the 1980s, U.S. semiconductor firms dominated the market, though Japanese companies had appeared on the scene as real players by the late 1970s, as demand for semiconductors shifted away from U.S. government defense and space purchases toward consumer electronics and other commercial applications. In the mid-1980s, consumer electronics accounted for almost half of semiconductor demand in Japan, while data processing accounted for 44 percent of U.S. demand.

At the end of the 1970s, American firms accounted for 60 percent of the world market and the Japanese less than 30 percent. By 1985, both countries held world market shares of about 45 percent, with the Japanese moving to a position of leadership. Most Japanese inroads came in dynamic random access memory (DRAM) computer chips, the natural entrée point (as it would be later for Korea) because of the straightforward design technology compared to other semiconductor devices. In DRAMs, by the mid-1980s Japan had completely reversed positions with the United States, controlling 70 percent of the world market, a percentage held by the United States in the late 1970s (Flamm 1996; Irwin 1998).

The crisis was precipitated by a number of factors, including in the background a high U.S. dollar that greatly undermined U.S. export capacity and decreased fixed investment because of the high cost of capital. Then a substantial boom in the semiconductor market from 1983 to 1984 quickly turned into a deep industry recession in 1985, triggered largely by a slump in computer sales. The DRAM market contracted by 60 percent. Interestingly, the recession itself was the chief cause of the

25

grief that came to U.S. semiconductor manufacturers. Three quarters of the decline in revenue in the mid-1980s stemmed from declining overall demand; only one quarter came from lost market share.

This boom and bust cycle remains a defining characteristic of the semiconductor industry, with the main variation being that individual product life cycles have become ever shorter and price fluctuation ever wider over time. Typically, several years after a bust, demand once again swells suddenly, often unexpectedly, and DRAM manufacturers all scramble to increase capacity in order to maintain market share. In the end, a glut of chips has once again been produced—or there is a shift in demand to a more advanced or different technology. Then the market crashes again, accompanied by the cyclical dumping described above. Because inventory and technology become obsolete very quickly, semiconductor producers cannot simply sit out the down periods of the cycle—they must continue to produce and invest heavily in R&D even during a downturn in order to meet the increased demand for new technology when the cycle turns up again. Predictably, this subjects them to serious financial problems.

In 1985, irrespective of these economic realities, huge pressures rose for the U.S. government to counter Japanese "predatory practices." Though the semiconductor trade association never achieved consensus on anti-dumping actions, individual companies mounted suits against particular semiconductor chip technologies: In an unprecedented step, the Commerce Department self-initiated a case against Japanese makers of DRAMs. Commerce's preliminary determination found high dumping margins, and the USITC also quickly reached an affirmative decision of material injury against U.S. companies.

Japan capitulated in the summer of 1986 and on July 30 signed the infamous Semiconductor Trade Agreement (STA) with the United States in return for suspension of the dumping actions. Under the STA, Japan agreed to take steps to end alleged dumping into the U.S. market, and Japanese firms agreed to supply price and sales data on a monthly basis to the Commerce Department (Flamm 1996; Dick 1995; Lindsey 1992; Irwin 1996).

The Ministry of International Trade and Industry (MITI) actually had no statutory authority to force Japanese firms to reduce production, and initially it had trouble getting them to comply with its request, which included a target of 10 percent reduction over a short period. In April 1987, however, the United States strengthened MITI's hand when it unleashed a stunning tariff retaliation (100 percent tariffs on Japanese electronics merchandise, including DRAMs). At that point, Japanese semiconductor firms fell into line and, in effect, MITI put together a government-led cartel. As the ultimate Japan basher of the time, Clyde Prestowitz, admitted, "For the free traders of the United States to be asking Japan to cartelize its industry was the supreme irony" (Prestowitz 1989, 167).

As with supercomputers and flat-panel displays, in this case the result of wielding the heavy-handed weapon of antidumping policy had both negative and unintended consequences. In the year after the STA, DRAM prices skyrocketed, and Japanese semiconductor companies went along for the ride because, as Prestowitz again stated, "The Japanese government force[d] its companies to make a profit" (Prestowitz 1989, 167).

Actually, they were already making a profit—what the STA did was to force them to make a "super profit." A Brookings Institution study estimated that extra profits on 1M DRAM sales for Japanese producers was $1.2 billion in 1988 alone and between $3 and $4 billion on all devices in 1989. This represented a direct transfer of money from U.S. consumers and U.S. companies dependent on semiconductor chips for their final products. Aware that the STA had instantly made them much less competitive against Japanese firms in the world market, the U.S. computer industry promptly established its own organization in order to counter the negative competitive effects of government policy (Flamm 1996).

The action also did not save American semiconductor companies, all of which left the DRAM market within a decade, with the exception of Micron Technology. What the U.S. action did accomplish, however, was to accelerate the entrance of Korean companies onto the world DRAM scene—as with Japanese companies, the supernormal profits that were obtainable in the years immediately after the U.S.-Japan agreement allowed Korean firms such as Hyundai, Samsung, and LG to reap unexpected returns and gain a foothold at the lower end of the semiconductor technology ladder. This was a very expensive way to increase world competition, however, and provide additional DRAM sources for U.S. computer companies (Yoon 1992; Irwin 1998).

Further, in terms of historical lessons, it is clear in retrospect that once again U.S. government officials, including the Pentagon, wholly misunderstood the technological trajectory of a high-tech industry. A Defense Science Board report in 1987 stated firmly that DRAMs were the key to future U.S. technology leadership—a central element of the "technology food chain," and that loss of the DRAM industry would cripple the ability of U.S. firms to compete in all other high-tech electronic sectors (U.S. Department of Defense 1987). What the Defense Science Board and other policy entrepreneurs pushing industrial policy for the United States did not understand was that American companies had already discerned that DRAMs were becoming a high-volume, low-profit commodity and that the wave of the future for U.S. firms was in more advanced microprocessors and specialty chips, along with chip design rather than actual production.

Finally, the mantra of U.S. government officials, corporate leaders, and purveyors of gloom and doom about America's technological future during the entire period had been the necessity to dismantle "Japan, Inc." and with it MITI's alleged control of Japanese industries. But the STA had just the opposite effect: it allowed MITI officials, who actually had been losing control of Japanese multinationals, to reassert their authority. For it was MITI that divided the spoils by setting the production targets for individual companies, and it was MITI that monitored prices so that high rates of profit would be maintained. As Kenneth Flamm of the Brookings Institution (often a supporter of activist policies for semiconductors) subsequently stated:

> Contradictions between tactical compromises and strategic, long-run principles in U.S. trade policy ultimately [came] home to roost. Having failed to achieve function access to the Japanese market in the mid-1970s, after formal trade barriers were removed, the United States essentially decided to use the informal system of MITI guidance and government collaboration with an industrial inner circle to achieve an outcome that at least resembled what it thought real system reform might have accomplished. Paradoxically, this decision probably strengthened what had been waning MITI influence in the Japanese semiconductor industry. . . . Rather than supporting a system that would guarantee real competition in global markets for high-technology products, the United States [came] to wear the mantle of defender of the status quo. (Flamm 1996, 457–458)

Postscript

From 1990 to 1995, U.S. fortunes in the semiconductor sector reversed and worldwide, for all types of chips and microprocessors, U.S. firms regained parity with Japan and producers from other nations. Japan remained an important presence in DRAMs, but most observers take this lingering hold on a comparatively low-technology chip as a telling sign that—in contrast to the dire predictions of the mid-1980s—Japan has fallen far behind the United States in many segments of the high-tech end of electronics.

Still, old habits die hard. During the entire decade, one of the two surviving U.S. DRAM manufacturers, Micron, whose sales had jumped sixfold during the STA crisis, continued to attempt to use U.S. antidumping laws as a competitive tool, abetted as always by U.S. trade and commercial officials. In April 1992, Micron filed an antidumping suit against the new boys on the block, the Koreans—Hyundai Electronics, Samsung, and LG Semicon (LGS). The Department of Commerce (DOC) found small dumping margins, and a year later a deeply divided USITC declared that the domestic U.S. industry suffered material damage (U.S. International Trade Commission 1993).

Three years later, Samsung, the largest Korean DRAM manufacturer, won an appeal against the DOC's determination, resulting in its removal from the antidumping order (U.S. Department of Commerce 1995, 1996). This left the order standing only against Hyundai (which later in 1999 took over LGS). Subsequently, the Commerce Department's annual reviews of Hyundai's prices found no continuing evidence of dumping for three straight years; it still refused to lift the original 1993 dumping order (U.S. Department of Commerce 1999).

Micron continued its strategic use of antidumping laws by filing suit against Taiwanese DRAM producers in October 1998. Dutifully, Commerce found dumping margins of 8 to 69 percent, but then, in a surprising but economically sound decision, the USITC ruled that Micron and other U.S. producers were *not* being injured or even threatened with injury by Taiwanese imports (U.S. International Trade Commission 1999a). As a result of this decision, the only outstanding U.S. government antidumping action against foreign manufacturers in the semiconductor industry was the anomalous order still pending against Hyundai.

At the end of 1999, U.S. trade officials at the Commerce Department and the International Trade Commission began a "sunset review" of the antidumping order against Hyundai, under new rules negotiated during the Uruguay Round, which mandate that WTO members review all antidumping orders after they have been in place for five years. The aim of a sunset review is to determine whether revocation would lead to either continued dumping or injury to the U.S. industry. The broader review relates to material injury because the USITC will examine a number of factors such as the composition of the industry, effects on prices and volume of imports, likely production shifts, and a kind of catchall, the overall impact on American producers.

With respect to the antidumping duty order on DRAMs from Korea, the International Trade Commission never completed its sunset review analysis because Micron essentially gave up in the middle of the proceeding. Just as the USITC was about to begin its final analysis, Micron submitted a letter to the Commerce Department stating that it no longer opposed termination of the antidumping duty order. As a result of Micron's letter, the Commerce Department found that no domestic party had an interest in continuing the antidumping duty order and therefore revoked it (U.S. Department of Commerce 2000).

Micron's decision to "sue for peace" before the USITC's analysis was not surprising. Any economic analysis of the competitive realities of the worldwide semiconductor industry in the late 1990s—whether conducted as a part of a sunset review or for *de novo* antidumping proceedings— would lead directly to the conclusion not only that this particular antidumping duty order was unwarranted, but also that the entire rationale behind antidumping actions for this industry is flawed and inevitably results in a reduction of world economic welfare. The following sections will explain why this is so.

Internationalization and Consolidation of the Semiconductor Industry

What a difference a decade makes. As we have seen, in the early 1990s, it was widely predicted that Japan would dominate the semiconductor market and that U.S. companies would permanently exit the sector— and no one paid much attention to upstarts like Korea or Taiwan. Today, Japanese companies are leaving DRAMs behind; one U.S. company, Micron, has become the world technology leader, and the Koreans, followed by the Taiwanese, have become major players.

In the semiconductor industry as a whole, American companies regained home market shares after the mid-1990s: In 1995, domestic company production was about 60 percent of the total U.S. semiconductor market, but by the end of the 1990s, this share had increased and stabilized at just over 70 percent. At the same time, Japan's share of the semiconductor market, both globally and in the United States, declined dramatically and was replaced by Korea in most markets. Japan's global market share fell from 46 percent in 1991 to 28 percent in 2001; by 2001, Japan's share of the U.S. market had dropped to 11 percent. Third-country producers (largely Korean and European) had increased world market share to over 20 percent by the late 1990s (Cooney 2003; Manyin, Cooney, and Grimmette 2003).

TABLE 1
MAJOR DRAM PRODUCERS IN THE MID-1990S

Country	DRAM Producers
United States	IBM, Motorola, Micron, Texas Instruments
Japan	NEC, Matsushita, Mitsubishi, Hitachi, Toshiba
Korea	Samsung, Hyundai, LG Semiconductor
Europe	Siemens, Phillips

DRAMs. As with the overall semiconductor industry, the recent history of DRAM producers has been characterized by consolidation and internationalization. The accompanying tables demonstrate the major changes within the industry over the past several years. Up until the mid-1990s, there were ten DRAM producers with more than 5 percent of world market share (Table 1).

By 2001, the top four DRAM manufacturers controlled 80 percent of the market.

In the United States, the driving force behind the consolidation was the decision of a number of high-end electronic companies to exit the commodity DRAM market in favor of manufacturing more sophisticated and flexible chips and integrated circuits. The consolidation began in 1998 when Micron bought out Texas Instruments' (TI's) semiconductor business. It continued over the next several years, with both IBM and Motorola deciding to get out of DRAM production. IBM sold its share in a joint venture with Toshiba (which in turn sold out to Micron), and Motorola sold its share in a joint venture to its partner, Infineon (Cooney 2003).

Boom and Bust. Outside of the United States, the 1997 Asian financial crisis and then the 2000–2001 "dot.com" crash and the ensuing worldwide economic slowdown drastically accelerated an industry shakeout in Asia. The 2000–2001 crash was the deepest in the history of the semiconductor industry, with worldwide sales falling one-third, or $66 billion. Capacity utilization dropped to 65 percent by the end of 2001, before rebounding to about 75 percent in 2002, largely as a result of plants being taken out of production (Cooney 2003). Japan's economy, which experienced four recessions during the 1990s, was a continual drag on Japanese semiconductor companies even before the onset of the 1997 crisis. With regard to the hitherto highly successful Korean firms, the combination of the crippling blows delivered by the financial crisis of

TABLE 2
WORLDWIDE DRAM MARKET SHARES, 1999, 2000, AND 2001

	1999	2000	2001
Micron	14.4%	18.9%	19.1%
Infineon	7.3%	8.5%	9.7%
Hynix	19.3%	17.2%	14.5%
Samsung	20.7%	21.1%	27.0%
All others	38.2%	34.4%	29.7%

Source: Dataquest 2002.

1997 and the "dot.com" bust just two years later forced a wholesale restructuring.

After the 1997 Asian crisis, strong growth and demand for DRAMs continued in the still burgeoning U.S. market, and producers worldwide hugely increased capacity and production. But if the run-up of demand and prices was swift, so was the crash. DRAM prices peaked in early 2000 at twelve to thirteen dollars per chip, but by the end of that year had fallen as low as ninety cents to one dollar per chip. Over the next eighteen months, virtually all DRAM manufacturers were producing chips at a substantial loss. Because of the technological/competitive imperatives described above, each individual company refrained from temporarily halting production or lowering prices, hoping that other companies with less economic strength would be forced to exit the market. By the end of 2001, the clear losers were Japanese producers, and just four major companies remained as major players in the global DRAM market (Table 2).

Samsung emerged as the worldwide leader in DRAM sales (27 percent), followed by Micron (19.1 percent), Hynix (14.5 percent), and Infineon (9.7 percent). Micron and the smaller Infineon seemed to have benefited most by the shakeout, gaining together about a 7 percent increase in worldwide sales. As noted below, Hynix was created in 1999 by the merger and spinoff of the DRAM plants of Hyundai and the LG Group in Korea. Infineon was a spinoff from Siemens in Europe and, though smaller than other producers, is attempting to build important alliances with Taiwanese firms such as Nanya, Winbond, and Promos Technologies. And as for Japan, it had now largely left the competition to others: Toshiba exited the DRAM market in 2000, and Hitachi and NEC had combined their operations in a new, much smaller spinoff company, Elpida, which is competing with Infineon for key Taiwanese alliances (Willkie Farr & Gallagher 2002; Manyin, Cooney, and Grimmett 2002). As

TABLE 3
U.S. DRAM MARKET SHARES, 1999, 2000, AND 2001

	1999	2000	2001
Micron	21.0%	27.0%	26.2%
Infineon	6.7%	7.4%	11.5%
Hynix	15.2%	13.6%	10.6%
Samsung	22.5%	23.7%	28.3%
All others	34.6%	28.4%	23.4%

Source: Dataquest 2002.
Note: Hynix and Samsung include non-subject U.S. production.

Table 3 shows, the U.S. market generally mirrored the world market, though in the U.S. market, Micron replaced Samsung as the leader in sales in 2000.

Finally, even with the dramatic shakeout, the DRAM industry remains a global one, with each major company supporting R&D and production facilities around the world. In the United States, for instance, all of the major competitors with Micron maintain important production plants: Samsung (Texas), Hynix (Oregon), and Infineon (Virginia). And in a true "world turned upside down" phenomenon, since 1999 KMT Semiconductor (Micron's joint venture with Kobe Steel) has become a leading DRAM producer in Japan. Table 4 lists the various facilities of the major DRAM producers around the world.

Micron. Over the past half decade, Micron's world has also changed dramatically, with important consequences for current and future U.S. antidumping policy toward semiconductors. Long called the "America First" DRAM maker and noted for its aggressive use of antidumping laws as a competitive tool, since the late 1990s Micron has been catapulted onto the world scene as a major player with the acquisition of TI's manufacturing plants in Italy, Japan, Scotland, and Singapore. This is a startling development for a company whose international operations as late as mid-1998 consisted of sixty workers in sales offices scattered around Asia and the United Kingdom. By 2002, more than 50 percent of Micron's DRAM production was outside of the United States (Industry Trade Reports 1997–2000).

At the present time, Micron, Infineon, and Samsung are in a heated contest for technological leadership. By the end of 2002, more than 50 percent of Micron's capacity in DRAM production was expected to come from

TABLE 4

LOCATION OF MAJOR DRAM PRODUCERS' MANUFACTURING FACILITIES, 2002

	Manufacturing Locations	Activity	Established	Ownership
Micron	Boise, Idaho, USA	Production	1981	Full
	Avezzano, Italy	Production	1998	Full
	Singapore, Singapore	Production	1998	JV[6] with Canon, Hewlett Packard, Singapore Gov.
	Singapore, Singapore	A&T[4]	1998	Full
	East Kilbride, Scotland	A&T	2000	Full
	Lehi, Utah, USA[5]	A&T	2000	Full
	Nishiwaki City, Japan	Production	2001	Full
	Manassas, Virginia, USA	Production	2002	Full
Infineon[1]	Malacca, Malaysia	A&T	n.a.	Full
	Hsinchu, Taiwan	Production	1997	JV with MoselVitelic
	Porto, Portugal	A&T	1998	Full
	Richmond, Virginia, USA	Production	1998	Full
	Dresden, Germany	Production	1999	JV with Motorola
	Corbeil, France	Production	1999	JV with IBM
	Taouyen, Taiwan	Production	Late 2003	JV (50:50) with Nanya
Hynix[2]	Ichon, Korea	Production	1983	Full
	Eugene, Oregon, USA	Production	1996	Full
	Cheongju, Korea	Production	1999	Full
	Kumi, Korea	Production	1999	
Samsung[3]	Kiheung, Korea	Production	1983	Full
	Onyang, Korea	A&T	1990	Full
	Austin, Texas, USA	Production	1998	JV, with Intel (Intel owns less than 10%)
	Hwasung, Kyunggi-do, Korea	Production	2000	Full
	Suzhou, China	A&T	To expand to DRAMs in 2003	Full

(1) Source: Infineon Technology 2002.
(2) Source: Mr. S. W. Kim, swkim@hsma.us.hynix.com, (541)338-5000, Strategic Planning Manager, Eugene, Oregon, USA.
(3) Source: Samsung Electronics 2002.
(4) A&T = Assembly and Testing
(5) The facility at Lehi, Utah, will be converted into a manufacturing facility "when it makes sense to do so according to prevailing market conditions" Source: Mr. Sean Mahoney, smahoney@micron.com, (208) 368-3127, Media Relations, Boise, Idaho, USA.
(6) JV = Joint Venture

advanced .13-micron technology, while Infineon has made 100 percent conversion of chipmaking to .14-micron technology. Since the TI acquisition, Micron has moved aggressively to retool all of its newly acquired plants with the latest advances in chip-making (Willkie Farr & Gallagher 2002; Manyin, Cooney, and Grimmett 2003).

Second, industry experts point out that as a bonus from the TI acquisition, Micron mastered one lesson of international competition without even trying. TI had done the necessary homework for placing plants strategically—near its customers—around the world. In Singapore, for instance, Hewlett-Packard and Dell build PCs using Micron chips; and the Micron plant in Scotland is a forty-minute drive from Compaq, Hewlett-Packard, and Sun Microsystems plants.

Policy Lessons

If Micron's transition from a national to a multinational company is the stuff of business school casebooks, it also presents fascinating challenges to the company in the public policy arena and the question—in the words of Jack Robertson, one of the keenest reporters observing the industry—of whether the company might "soften its feisty stand on some international issues" (Robertson 1998, 4).

Taiwan's 1998 actions on antidumping issues are a good case in point on this question. After Micron filed an antidumping claim against Taiwanese companies in that year, the Taiwanese responded almost immediately with a counterclaim that Micron was dumping in Taiwan's market. Later, after the United States found that Taiwanese companies were not injuring the U.S. semiconductor industry, the Taiwanese government reversed a preliminary decision of guilt and dropped the case. It was clear that Taiwan was now quite prepared to play the antidumping card against U.S. companies in response to actions against its own companies. (In 2003, with even greater protection against U.S counter-retaliation afforded by its new membership in the WTO, it is likely that Taiwan will become even more aggressive in wielding the antidumping weapon.)

As noted earlier, the spread of antidumping actions around the world—targeting the United States and Europe particularly—is coming back to haunt U.S. companies that repeatedly used the U.S. trade remedy laws as tools to beat back more efficient competitors. Though Micron escaped an adverse action, in recent years other major U.S. companies

(Dow Chemical, Exxon, 3M, International Paper, USX, Frigidaire, Union Carbide, Whirlpool, Bristol-Myers, and Squibb, just to name a few) have felt the sting (and lost sales) from antidumping actions in foreign markets (Lindsey and Ikenson 2001).

Second, given the global nature of the semiconductor industry at this point—manufacturing facilities for each of the major DRAM producers dotted around the world—it is preposterous to argue that the conditions that produce dumping are likely or even possible (that is, the existence of a protected sanctuary market from which producers can export at below-cost prices, while making up the difference at home). Samsung, Hynix, and Infineon all produce DRAMs in the United States, thus precluding monopoly pricing and export dumping by Micron. Conversely, why would any of the foreign producers "dump" in the U.S. market, thereby undercutting the competitiveness of its own U.S. plant?

The third lesson stems from quite recent events. Leading U.S. firms in sectors such as steel and semiconductors have "cried wolf" so often in trying to get the U.S. government to invoke trade remedy laws in their defense that when a potentially legitimate complaint arises, they face major credibility problems. Such is the case in the unfolding dispute over a series of rescue packages over the past two years that have kept the Korean semiconductor company Hynix in business by continually allowing it to restructure its debt of $6.5 billion.

Hynix: A Legitimate Use of Countervailing Duties Against Subsidies?
The issues concern the degree to which the Korean government was involved in these rescues and whether this involvement constituted a violation of WTO subsidy rules. Behind these public policy questions lies a private market puzzle of whether Hynix faces such intractable structural deficiencies that it will not survive in world competition.

Hynix was created in 1999 by the merger of a Hyundai spinoff (also named Hynix) with the DRAM components of the LG Semiconductor company. In sealing the merger, Hynix took on over $4 billion in debt from the LG Semiconductor company, in addition to its own inherited debt from Hyundai. As a result of this outsized debt (and the fact that Hyundai stripped the new company of substantial cash reserves), Hynix was particularly vulnerable to the crash that occurred in the worldwide DRAM market in late 2000 (Manyin, Cooney, and Grimmett 2003).

Even before the bottom fell out, Hynix had benefited from a government-led assistance package for its parent company, Hyundai. In January 2000, the state-owned Korea Development Bank organized a $1 billion aid plan for several of the Korean *chaebol* (conglomerates) that were about to default on their debts; and Hynix was the beneficiary of some of this direct state intervention. Subsequently, Hynix creditor Korean banks— with small contributions by non-Korean financial institutions such as Citibank and Commerzbank, which also hold debt from the company— have constructed three separate "assistance packages." These restructuring actions, which occurred in May and October 2001 and again in December 2002, included some new funds but largely consisted of deals to roll over existing debt or repackage it with debt for equity swaps. As a result of the latest December 2002 bailout, Hynix debts have been rescheduled to come due in 2006, and creditors now own two-thirds of the company (*Financial Times [FT]* December 9, 13, 31, 2002; Interview, James P. Durling, in Willkie Farr & Gallagher 2002; Manyin, Cooney, and Grimmett 2003).

In addition, matters had been further complicated in the spring of 2002 when negotiations began for Micron to take over the Hynix DRAM business. Under a deal announced in April, Micron would acquire this business for $3.4 billion in cash and Micron stock transfers. The offer garnered the support of the Korean government and Hynix's creditors, but Hynix's board of directors vetoed the plan at the last moment, arguing that the sale price amounted to a fire sale and a recent increase in world chip prices would give Hynix the means of surviving alone. Subsequently, Micron stated it no longer had any interest in acquiring Hynix or any of its individual pieces (Interview, James P. Durling, in Willkie Farr & Gallagher 2002; *FT* December 9 and 13, 2002).

From the time of the first government-led bailout in January 2000, Micron and the U.S. government, as well as Infineon and the EU, have strongly protested that such rescue packages violate WTO subsidy rules and constitute unfair trade practices under both U.S. and EU law. In June 2002, Infineon filed a countervailing duty case against Hynix (and Samsung, for good measure) with the EU. In November 2002, at the behest of Micron a similar suit was filed against both companies in the United States. The United States and the EU are also taking steps to file a WTO complaint, arguing that the bailouts violate the WTO Agreement on Subsidies and Countervailing Measures (SCM) (Manyin, Cooney, and Grimmett 2003; *FT* December 31, 2002).

Defenders of Hynix point out that the initial January 2000 government intervention was not directed solely at DRAM producers but more generally at the entire Korean manufacturing sector, and the bond refinancing was at then-market rates. The Korean government avers that it did not pressure the banks to bail out the company in the subsequent rollovers and cash infusions. It also points out that foreign banks such as Citibank and Commerzbank supported the 2001–2002 rescue efforts—and that some Korean banks refused to participate in the bailouts. In order to avoid further exposure, they simply wrote off their loans and accepted 75 percent losses (Durling 2002).

Against this defense, critics (both governments and private sector competitors) claim it was no coincidence the consortia that organized the package were composed of "private" banks either owned outright or controlled by the Korean government, as a result of nationalization during the Asian financial crisis (90 percent of the new loans given to Hynix came from banks in which the government was the largest stockholder). Looking at the broader context of the Korean economy's operation, critics point out that for decades, Korean banks have operated as financial arms of the government, with credit allocation based not upon risk assessment but upon political connections. In an interview with the *Financial Times* after the announcement of the most recent bailout, Steve Appleton, chairman and CEO of Micron, charged that "since 1998, Hynix has received $11 billion in various forms of subsidies. It's like the movie, *Groundhog Day*. Every day, we are competing against a company that is subsidized by a government. We can compete against any company in the world but not against governments. Market principles should come into play" (*FT* December 13, 2002; see also *FT* December 9, 2002; Manyin, Cooney, and Grimmett 2002).

Ironically, whatever the legal and political outcome of the various cases, the market and technological imperatives may ultimately dictate the final outcome in this instance. As outside observers have noted, the realities of the DRAM business cycle may finally defeat Hynix. Over the past two years, its financial problems have prevented key investment in the technological improvements and upgraded equipment it must employ in order to compete in the next upturn in demand and prices. According to most estimates, Hynix's investments in upgrading and new technology amount to less than one-quarter of that plowed back by Samsung and Micron. Thus, at some point over the next few years, Hynix could well be back on the auction block, forcing another test of the Korean government's nonintervention resolve.

7

Steel

The U.S. Steel Industry: Obsolescence and Technological Resurgence

The U.S. steel industry would in many ways seem to fit oddly into the themes and examples in this study. But the history of this industry illustrates another important phenomenon: In order to survive and prosper, traditional manufacturing in advanced industrial economies (steel, textiles, chemicals, as examples) must continually move up the technological ladder and ultimately find niches where the combination of new technological processes and a highly skilled labor force provides the means to retain a comparative advantage over less-developed economies. Advances such as computer-assisted design and manufacturing in the textile industry, and electric-arc furnaces and Steckel mill technology in the steel industry, have thus allowed smaller but highly efficient traditional industries to survive in the United States and other advanced economies.

Unfortunately, the highly protectionist use of trade remedy laws has dampened and slowed this healthy adjustment process in the U.S. steel industry. As the accompanying table illustrates, for three decades the American steel industry has been the most prolific user of these protectionist tools (Table 5). Ultimately a failure as a means of saving obsolete segments of the U.S. steel industry, antidumping and countervailing actions have also impeded the emergence of a high-tech U.S. steel minimill industry that can compete in world markets for many steel products.

The U.S. Steel Industry since 1945. In many ways, the U.S. steel industry was a victim of the overwhelming U.S. victory in the Second World War and the quick onset of the Cold War almost immediately thereafter. During World War II, the U.S. government had underwritten the construction of huge new steel capacity (15 million new tons annually) as part of the war mobilization effort. The outbreak of the Korean War and the subsequent Cold War defense effort brought an additional expansion of some

TABLE 5
SHARE OF U.S. STEEL AD/CVD CASES (1973–2002) IN ABSOLUTE NUMBERS

Years	Total AD Cases	AD Cases on Steel Products	Total CVD Cases	CVD Cases on Steel Products
1973–1979	8	2	1	0
1980–1984	9	1	1	0
1985–1989	51	20	9	5
1990–1994	66	33	12	9
1995–1999	54	27	10	7
2000–2002	70	40	18	12
Total	258	123	51	33

Source: Author's calculations.

40 million tons by 1960. These pressures—and opportunities—in a U.S. market as yet unchallenged by foreign operations led to the first of many strategic technological errors. (Sources for the postwar history of the U.S. steel industry described in this study include: Barnett and Schorsch 1983; Hogan 1994; Tiffany 1988; Tornell 1997; Barringer and Pierce 2000.)

In meeting the great new demands of the U.S. defense and civilian markets, U.S. steel makers opted for two pathways: expanding existing but already obsolete open-hearth furnaces (OHF); and attempting to graft the more advanced basic oxygen furnace (BOF) onto old mills, many of which dated back to the nineteenth century. Though much less costly to bring online (roughly 75 percent), the expanded OHF and fused-BOF mills were both technologically inferior and much less efficient than if new mills wholly adapted to the new BOF technology had been constructed. (OHF furnaces use an external source of heat that can take up to six hours to reach maximum heat efficiency; in contrast, BOF furnaces produce this maximum efficiency in forty minutes by injecting oxygen into a holding vessel containing iron, scrap, and lime and allowing the oxygen to interact with the iron to generate the necessary heat.) As late as 1960, outmoded OHF technology accounted for 90 percent of domestic steel's total capacity—and by that time both Europe and Japan had rebuilt their steel industries at "greenfield sites" utilizing the latest steel-making technologies (Hogan 1994).

The decision to add capacity at existing sites in the East and Midwest meant that the plants were remote from Pacific Coast states, where demand exploded after the war—thus increasing the logistical costs of shipping and customer service. Other transportation and logistical advances outside the

United States further undermined U.S. international competitiveness. U.S. steel makers long enjoyed a cost advantage because of their proximity to coal and iron ore deposits, but by the early 1970s the discovery of high-quality iron deposits outside the United States (in Australia and Brazil), combined with the introduction of new ocean-going bulk tankers, drastically reduced this advantage. One study has estimated that between 1958 and 1980, by sourcing low-cost ore and using huge bulk carriers, Japan turned a 28 percent cost disadvantage on steel raw materials into a 30 percent advantage (Barnett and Schorsch 1983).

From the late 1960s through the 1970s, European and Japanese competitors also outdistanced U.S. companies by early adoption of another major technological breakthrough in steel making: continuous casting. Continuous casting represented a big advance over the ingot casting technology that had been utilized since the days of Andrew Carnegie. In ingot casting, raw molten steel is poured into a mold, allowed to cool into an ingot, then transported to a rolling facility where the ingot is reheated and transformed into a slab, which is finally rolled into a finished product. Continuous casting eliminates all of the steps from raw steel to slab by channeling the raw steel directly from a furnace to a casting machine that molds the steel into the slab form, after which it can be shaped into a finished product. As late as 1980, only 20 percent of U.S. facilities used continuous casting, while over 60 percent of Japanese plants had installed the new technology; in 1989, the U.S. figure had risen to 65 percent, but the totals for Japan and the EU were 93 percent and 88 percent, respectively (Tornell 1997; Barringer and Pierce 2000).

Industrial Structure, Capital Markets, and Labor Relations

While technology constituted the exogenous driving force in the postwar history of the steel industry, in each national economy it interacted differentially with other factors, such as industrial structure (conditions of competition), capital markets, labor relations, and last but not least, the role of government. In the immediate postwar United States, eight large integrated steel makers which operated through time-honored oligopolistic tactics dominated the U.S. steel industry. Rather than investing in new technologies and innovative new products, they often sought super-normal profits (rents, in economists' terms) through price collusion (Acs 1984).

Price collusion was directly linked with labor relations. For two decades after 1945, each year Big Steel, in what was dubbed the annual "rites of spring," would agree to sizable wage increases with the United Steelworkers Union and then announce increased steel prices. (From 1947 to 1957, average wage increases were 6.6 percent, and average steel price increases were 7 percent.) In addition, relations between management and labor remained poisonous throughout the period, and five major strikes occurred between 1945 and 1960. Two rules regarding labor relations in the industry contributed to the turmoil and outsized wage increases: one allowed reopening of wage talks at any time during a contract, and the second provided for industry-wide bargaining, resulting in total industry shutdowns at almost any time the workers at one plant decided to strike (Hoerr 1988). This highly disruptive pattern first caused U.S. steel users to look abroad for more stable (and cheaper) suppliers. During the 1960s, steel imports rose from 5 million tons to 18 million tons per year.

In 1973, in response to this outside threat, Big Steel and the labor unions agreed to a "no lockout, no strike" policy that mandated binding arbitration in labor disputes. Though resulting in relative labor peace, this new rule only exacerbated the competitiveness problems of the large, integrated steel companies. The agreement mandated arbitration of wage disputes and also provided for automatic cost-of-living increases for union members. Subsequently, in regard to union demands for wage increases beyond cost-of-living adjustments, arbitrators tended to split the difference, leading to an upward spiral of wages throughout the period. The result was that by 1977 the average wage of steelworkers was over 70 percent higher than the average of all U.S. manufacturing workers—and this figure climbed to 95 percent in the early 1980s (Crandall 1981).

Technological obsolescence and outmoded industrial practices and plants inevitably produced lower profits, a trend that caused capital markets to cast a jaundiced eye at the industry. A vicious cycle ensued in which the low return on investments made it difficult to issue new stock, finance long-term debt, or even retain enough earnings to finance R&D or badly needed investment in new capital stock and equipment. In a desperate attempt to break out of this cycle, during the late 1970s Big Steel launched major—and stunningly misguided—efforts to diversify into other industries (Tornell 1997; Barringer and Pierce 2000). These moves significantly drained what little retained earnings the companies had at their disposal away from plant and equipment upgrading and in the end resulted in a squandering of the money. U.S. Steel led the parade in 1982 when it acquired Marathon Oil for almost $6 billion—just at the time it was lobbying Congress hard for tax breaks to modernize its inefficient steel plants. U.S. Steel went on to invest in a chemical company, a domestic barge line, a dock company, and a gas utility. Other integrated companies also diversified into transportation, insurance, and savings and loan firms. (One telling additional factoid: in 1983, when U.S. Steel lost over $200 million in the first quarter alone, it still allocated over 80 percent of its capital expenditures to upgrading facilities at Marathon.)

Early Import Penetration. The combined effects described above of corporate mismanagement and retrograde technology left the U.S. steel industry ill-equipped to meet the challenge of international competition, when other European and Asian economies recovered in the two decades after 1945. Thus, even before the onslaught of the minimill revolution rocked U.S. steel companies, foreign steel came pouring across the border in increasing quantities. Between 1963 and 1983, imports of foreign steel increased from about 5 percent to 25 percent of total U.S. consumption. Much of this steel was lower-grade semifinished slabs that U.S. steel companies themselves imported because of their own inadequate raw-steel-making capacity *and* because it could be purchased more cheaply than they could make it. Increasingly, however, foreign steel imports competed for markets of more technologically refined steel products (Crandall 1981; Barringer and Pierce 2000).

The Gradual—but Decisive—Minimill Revolution

From their introduction in the late 1960s, minimills—utilizing a new electric arc furnace technology that transformed scrap steel into semifinished and later finished steel products—advanced slowly but steadily as competitors to Big Steel. Then they took off during the 1990s, as major new technological breakthroughs in their production processes allowed them to encroach dramatically on the high-end steel markets that had previously been the preserve of the integrated steel companies (Barnett and Crandall 1986; Tornell 1997). In 2002, minimills produced about 50 percent of all steel products in the United States. Despite the jingoistic, antiforeign rhetoric of Big Steel, minimills—rather than the Japanese, the Europeans, or the Koreans—were the real cause of decline of integrated steel makers.

Electric arc furnaces, which utilize scrap steel or scrap substitutes as their feedstock, generate heat through electric charges that leap between electrodes in the furnace lid. One scholar succinctly described the advantages and efficiencies of minimill technology:

> Minimill technology consists of pouring scrap into an electric furnace to produce molten steel. This process bypasses the processes of coking, palletizing and melting pig iron that are used in integrated plants. Since this process does not use blast furnaces of BOFs (which need a minimum plant size of 3 million tons per year), it realizes economies of scale at much lower production levels (less than one million tons per year). This reduces capital costs significantly. The other advantage of minimills is that because they are small, they can be located closer to each of their markets, thus reducing transport costs. (Tornell 1997, 14)

In their earliest form, minimills had a limited capacity of 250,000 to 500,000 tons annually—and technologically they were capable of producing only low-end (so-called long steel) products such as slabs, rods, and bars. The real minimill revolution, however, occurred during the 1990s, beginning in 1989 when Nucor Steel opened the world's first thin-slabbed, flat-rolling plant in Crawfordsville, Indiana. As the name implies, this new technology allowed for continuous casting of much thinner slabs—two inches—as compared with traditional slabs of eight to ten inches. Production of thinner slabs translated into much lower construction costs (from $1000 per ton of annual capacity to $200 per ton) and provided the impetus for minimill operators to compete directly in the flat-rolled market (steel for construction equipment and machine tools). For the first time, minimills could become "maximills" and reach capacities equal to those of Big Steel—up to 4–5 million tons of hot-rolled capacity per year. In addition, the efficiency costs per ton of steel now far outstripped those of traditional Big Steel plants: For 1997, one study estimated that the most efficient thin-slab minimills achieved labor productivity breakthroughs that were four times more efficient than the most efficient integrated mills (Tornell 1997). These numbers set off a wave of new minimill construction during the 1990s. From 1990 to 1998, while integrated mill capacity increased only 3.2 percent, minimill capacity expanded by 50 percent (Figure 2).

To complete the technological story—at least to date—in 1999, yet another breakthrough allowed the minimills to assault the summit of high-end steel making—the plate market. This came with the introduction of so-called Steckel technology, which (as with thin-slab flat-rolling technology for hot-rolled steel) greatly reduces the number of steps needed to produce steel plate from slabs. This enables minimills to transform more raw steel

FIGURE 2
GROWTH OF U.S. MINIMILL INDUSTRY, 1970–2003 (IN PERCENTAGE)

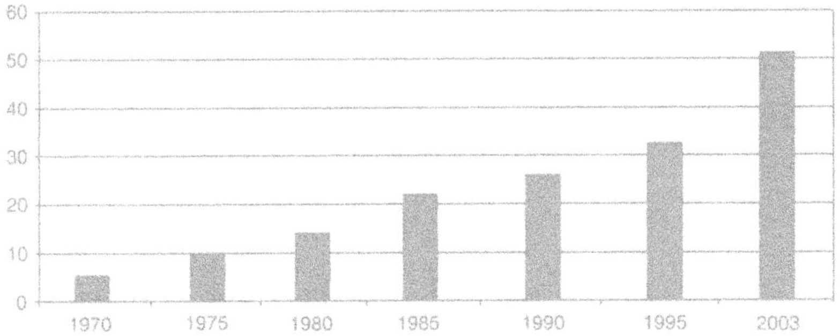

Source: Steel Manufacturers Association 2003a, 2003b.

into a finished product than conventional plants do, and reduces capital construction costs because the minimum scale (1–1.25 tons) is much lower than older plate technologies (Barringer and Pierce 2000).

In summary, minimills currently enjoy at least four advantages over Big Steel: one, lower labor costs due to the utilization of more advanced technology in steel making and the absence of front-end, labor-intensive coking and blast furnace operations; two, lower construction costs and reduced minimum scale of production have allowed minimill owners great flexibility in constructing new plants close to major markets in the Southeast and on the West Coast; three, lower capital costs have also allowed for a continuous, timely introduction of new productivity-enhancing technologies; and finally, newer "greenfield" plants have recruited a younger, more skilled, non-union work force and terminated many of the rigid work rules that impeded productivity advances in older, integrated plants.

The Role of Government: Protect and Subsidize

Ironically, even though the rise of domestic minimills provided the greatest competitive challenge to Big Steel, virtually all political animus was directed at "foreign steel," which, it was alleged from the late 1960s on, engaged in "unfair" competition against U.S. steel companies. Under the prodding of a powerful Steel Caucus in Congress, the federal government alternately (and sometimes simultaneously) protected and subsidized the domestic steel industry.

Government Subsidies. Foreign government subsidies have been repeatedly cited by the U.S. steel industry as a rationale for government aid and costly preferences in procurement. Yet it is rarely acknowledged that for the past thirty years, U.S. steel makers have received a steady stream of taxpayer-funds subsidies. The consulting firm Ernst and Young in 1989 estimated that to date, federal, state, and local government subsidies amounted to over $30 billion (Ernst and Young Consulting 1989). A more recent study, using more conservative assumptions and measurements, has calculated the combined total (through 1999) at over $16 billion (Barringer and Pierce 2000). A detailed accounting of these subsidies is beyond the purview of this study, but a list of the most prominent since the mid-1970s would include the following, in order of their estimated magnitude.

The most expensive cost to U.S. taxpayers has come from special exemptions from federal environmental regulations granted specifically to the steel industry, largely from the Clean Air Acts of 1981 and 1990. The 1981 Clean Air Act originally mandated the installation of new air pollution abatement equipment by December 1982. Through the intervention of the Steel Caucus, Congress granted steel companies a reprieve until December 1985, saving them almost $6 billion. In reaction to stringent proposed regulations against toxins generated by the coke ovens in the 1990 Clean Air Act, the steel companies and the Steel Caucus forced through a thirty-year "stretch out" provision that will save them another $4.5 billion (Barringer and Pierce 2000).

Steel companies (including minimills) have also greatly benefited from various "Buy American" acts. Under the provisions of these acts, foreign steel companies are foreclosed from competing for contracts in a number of highway construction, mass transit, pollution abatement, state and local public works, and airport construction programs. Over the past three decades, it is estimated that such subsidies have cost U.S. taxpayers over $4 billion.

Furthermore, responsibility for funding pension benefits has shifted from a number of steel companies to the federal government—that is, the Pension Benefit Guarantee Corporation, which was established as an insurance program against under- or nonfunded private pension programs. During the 1980s, particularly, a number of integrated steel companies, faced with huge unfounded pension liabilities, filed for bankruptcy and thus offloaded these liabilities to the federal government. The cost to taxpayers and other U.S. businesses through 1999 has been estimated at over $3.5 billion; however, the PBGC has recently announced it would take over the $3 billion liabilities of the bankrupt U.S. Steel Corporation, adding another large tranche of federal subsidies to this account (Sorkin 2003).

Over the past three decades, other notable subsidies to the steel industry include special federal tax exemptions, R&D grants, state and local tax exemptions, and—in 2000—a new federal loan guarantee program. Together, these additional subsidies add up to over $4.5 billion.

Finally, it should be noted that, as the steel companies endlessly proclaim, many foreign governments have also been guilty of wasteful subsidies of doubtful WTO legality. But at the same time, as the above narrative demonstrates, any move to introduce a truly "level playing field" worldwide—*sans* subsidies—would result in a wrenching adjustment for the steel industry in the United States, given its steady diet of government largesse for three decades.

Market Restrictions. In response to the first wave of foreign steel imports during the late 1960s, the steel industry and its allies in Congress forced the Nixon administration to negotiate a series of "voluntary" import restraints against Europe and Japan, after the United States threatened to enact a "surcharge" on steel imports. These restraints ran from 1969 to 1974. (This section of the study is gleaned from the following sources: Barfield 1999; Hufbauer and Goodrich 2001; Lindsey, Griswold, and Lukas 1999; Barringer and Pierce 2000.) Inexorably, however, because of the weak competitiveness of the technologically backward Big Steel companies, steel imports began to climb again under President Carter. Once again, trade restrictions became the first (and futile) line of defense, beginning with the filing of nineteen antidumping suits, followed by the establishment of a so-called trigger price mechanism (1978–1982), under which the federal government set a floor price on imported steel. When the Reagan administration abolished the trigger price scheme, the companies responded with a wave of over 100 antidumping suits, filed a Section 301 (unfair trade practices) suit alleging collusion between European and Japanese steel companies, and to gild the lily also filed a Section 201 escape clause action for emergency protection. The Reagan administration rejected both the Section 301 and the Section 201 requests; instead, it negotiated a series of "voluntary" import quotas on key steel products. These "voluntary" quotas lasted from 1982 to 1992.

For most of the 1990s, steel imports stabilized at about 20 percent of total U.S. production, but strong domestic demand for steel as a result of a booming U.S. economy muted calls for trade restrictions. This situation changed dramatically in 1998, and the years from 1998 to 2002 have been marked by downturn and turmoil in the U.S steel industry, resulting partly from foreign factors and partly from changes in the U.S. economy.

In 1998, the Asian financial crisis hit just as new producers from Russia and the former Soviet states began pushing new steel exports onto world markets. In the late 1990s, Southeast Asia was the largest regional steel market, importing some 75 million tons. All of Asia produced 300 million tons, or about 40 percent of world output. After the onset of the financial crisis, Southeast Asian consumption fell precipitously, and output was diverted to North America and Europe. As a result of political upheaval and cuts in military and civilian demand, producers in eastern Europe and the former Soviet bloc greatly increased exports and diverted those exports from Asia to the United States and Europe. Another factor that added to the pressure on the U.S. steel market was a large decrease in the value of many countries' currencies against the dollar, with declines ranging from 15 percent (Japan) to over 60 percent (Russia and Korea). In 1998 and early 1999, domestic factors in the U.S. market further made life difficult for U.S. companies: to wit, a sustained strike at General Motors sharply cut domestic demand and left domestic mills with significant overcapacity (Barfield 1999). But by the end of 1999, the markets had stabilized, prices rose, and steel imports leveled off at about 20 to 25 percent of total demand.

Then, to bring the story up to date, the dot.com crash and the ensuing downturn in the U.S. economy in 2000–2001 once again increased pressure on the steel industry. Capacity utilization dropped under 80 percent, and between 1998 and June 2003, forty steel companies filed for bankruptcy (Table 6). In addition, a major consolidation occurred in the integrated steel sector: International Steel Group acquired the assets of LTV Steel, Acme Metals, and Bethlehem Steel; U.S. Steel Corporation bought the assets of National Steel; Nucor Steel acquired the assets of Birmingham Steel and Trico Steel; and several producers of long steel merged to form Gerdau Ameristeel (Schneider 2003; USITC 2003a).

During this period, some 150 steel antidumping orders were in effect, covering almost 80 percent of all steel imports (Hufbauer and Goodrich

TABLE 6
U.S. STEEL INDUSTRY FILINGS FOR CHAPTER 11
BANKRUPTCY PROTECTION, 1998–2003

1998/99	Acme Metals	(9/29/98)
	Laclede Steel	(11/30/98)
	Geneva Steel	(2/1/99)
	Qualitech Steel SBQ	(3/24/99)
	Worldclass Processing	(3/24/99)
	Gulf States Steel	(7/1/99)
2000	J&L Structural Steel	(6/30/00)
	Vision Metals, Inc.	(11/13/00)
	Wheeling-Pittsburgh Steel	(11/16/00)
	Northwestern Steel and Wire	(12/20/00)
	Erie Forge and Steel	(12/22/00)
	LTV Corp.	(12/29/00)
2001	CSC Ltd.	(1/12/01)
	Heartland Steel	(1/24/01)
	GS Industries	(2/7/01)
	American Iron Reduction	(3/23/01)
	Trico Steel	(3/23/01)
	Republic Technologies	(4/2/01)
	Great Lakes Metals	(4/11/01)
	Freedom Forge (Standard Steel)	(7/13/01)
	Precision Specialty Metals	(7/16/01)
	Excaliber Holding Corp.	(7/18/01)
	Laclede Steel	(7/30/01)
	Edgewater Steel	(8/6/01)
	Riverview Steel	(8/7/01)
	GalvPro	(8/10/01)
	Bethlehem Steel	(10/15/01)
	Metals USA	(11/15/01)
	Sheffield Steel	(12/7/01)
	Action Steel	(12/28/01)
2002	Geneva Steel	(1/25/02)
	Huntco Steel	(2/4/02)
	National Steel	(3/6/02)
	Calumet Steel	(3/19/02)
	Birmingham Steel	(6/4/02)
	Cold Metal Products	(8/16/02)
	Geneva Steel Holdings (Geneva Steel's parent)	(9/13/02)
	Bayou Steel	(1/23/03)
2003	Kentucky Electric	(2/6/03)
	Slater Steel	(6/2/03)

Source: Association of Iron and Steel Engineers 2003.

FIGURE 3
U.S. DOMESTIC STEEL JOBS AND PRODUCTIVITY

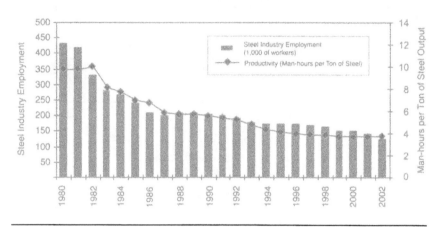

Source: American Iron and Steel Institute 2002.

2002). But in 2001, upon the arrival of the new Bush administration—with a narrow victory and heavy dependence (it seemed at the time) on retaining or capturing key steel states such as West Virginia, Ohio, and Michigan, in order to win reelection in 2004—the congressional Steel Caucus sharply increased pressure for even greater protective insurance. In March 2002, the Bush administration capitulated and invoked Section 201 of the basic U.S. trade act to impose "safeguards" in the form of tariffs of up to 30 percent on many steel imports, in addition to the existing antidumping orders (Barfield 2002).[4]

Steel and the State: Or the State of Steel, 2003

Now five decades after the Second World War, just what is the state of the U.S. steel industry, where does it stand in world competition, and what lessons can one take from the almost perpetual government intervention to save and foster this industry? The real drivers behind the changes in the U.S. steel industry's structure and employment are increased productivity through technological advance and the rise of the minimills—not unfair foreign competition, as spokesmen for the integrated steel companies continually assert.

As the above history and analysis have demonstrated, two steel industries now exist in the United States: one consisting of the older,

FIGURE 4
U.S. DOMESTIC STEEL SHIPMENTS AND IMPORT PERCENTAGE
OF APPARENT DOMESTIC CONSUMPTION, 1992–2002

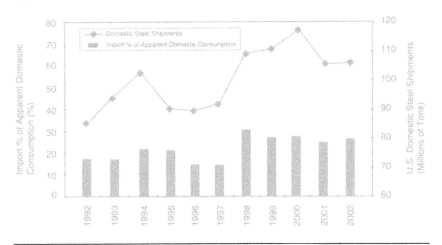

Source: U.S. Census Bureau 2003; American Iron and Steel Institute 2003.

increasingly uncompetitive integrated mills, and a second made up of more efficient, high-tech minimills. This reality must be kept in mind when dealing with all steel-related statistics. The accompanying figures illustrate this two-sided story.

Figure 3 shows a clear correlation between increased productivity and declining total employment in the steel industry: since 1980, the number of man-hours to produce a ton of steel in the United States has dropped by more than 50 percent, from ten man-hours in 1980 to less than four man-hours in 2002. Since U.S. basic demand for steel has not increased proportionally, fewer workers are required—a reality chronicled in the reduction of total U.S. steel jobs by almost two-thirds, from 435,000 in 1980 to 124,000 in 2002.

Total domestic shipments did increase, however, by some 25 percent between 1992 and 2002 (Figure 4)—thus reinforcing the argument that increased productivity, not declining total production, was one major cause of the decline in total steel employment. This decline will continue apace for the next decade. According to the U.S. Bureau of Labor Statistics, "Employment in the steel industry is expected to decline by about 22 percent over the 2000–2010 period, primarily due to increased use of labor-saving technologies and machinery. Other factors affecting

FIGURE 5
RELATIVE LABOR PRODUCTIVITY, 2001 (IN MAN HOUR/TON)

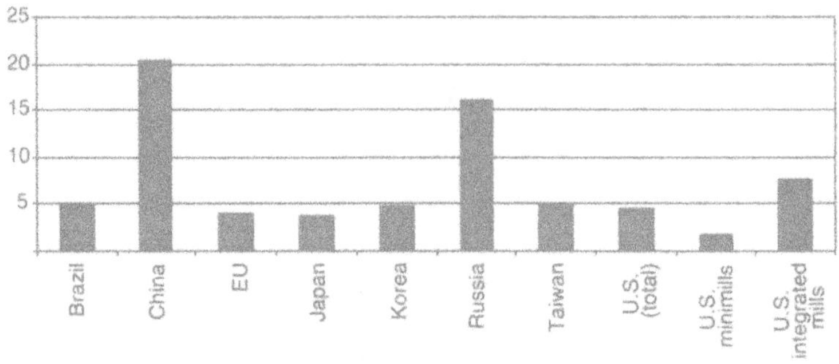

Source: World Steel Dynamics 2001.

employment in the industry include foreign trade, overall economic conditions, growth of EAFs [electric arc furnaces], and environmental regulations" (U.S. Bureau of Labor Statistics 2002, 80).

Though Figure 3 tells a story of huge increases in the productivity of the U.S. steel industry since 1980, Figure 5 reveals the real productivity leaders are the minimills, with the integrated firms lagging behind key U.S. competitors in man-hours per ton. While minimills take less than two man-hours to produce a ton of steel, the integrated mills take over seven man-hours to accomplish the same task.

Thus, as minimills climbed the technology ladder over the past two decades and competed increasingly for high-end finished products, they grabbed more and more of the U.S. domestic market.

Figure 2 traces the rise of minimills in the U.S. market since 1970. Meanwhile, as Figure 4 shows, the share of import foreign steel averaged 23 to 27 percent through the 1992–2002 period—kept down largely by the succession of antidumping countervailing duty orders chronicled in the previous sections.

In an ironic twist, considering the demand that Congress "Stand Up for Steel," U.S. integrated steel companies have over the past several decades become major importers of foreign steel, particularly low-end semifinished steel—slabs for steel sheet, billets for steel girders, and blooms for rebar. In 1998, integrated steel companies imported 6 million tons as inputs for more finished steel products (Lindsey, Griswold, and Lukas 1999).

TABLE 7
MAJOR STEEL-PRODUCING COUNTRIES, 2002
(MILLION METRIC TONS CRUDE STEEL PRODUCED)

Rank	Country	Tonnage	Rank	Country	Tonnage
1	China	181.6	6	South Korea	45.0
2	Japan	107.7	7	Ukraine	33.4
3	United States	92.2	8	India	29.6
4	Russia	59.8	9	Brazil	28.8
5	Germany	45.4	10	Italy	26.1
			—	World	902.2

Source: International Iron and Steel Institute 2003.

The World Market. Steel manufacturing has become global in nature. Once the domain of industrialized countries, it is now produced in fifty-six countries around the world, with the top five countries in 2002 (China, Japan, the United States, Russia, and Germany) accounting for only about 50 percent of total world production of crude steel (Table 7).

Although proximity to markets provides a competitive advantage, international steel trade has risen significantly over the past several decades; in many industrialized countries, including the United States, imports are a substantial component of domestic consumption. Despite the very large capacity of some steel operations, and mergers within and across borders, no individual producer or group dominates the global market. In 2002, the world's ten largest steel companies accounted for only a few percentage points of world production (Table 8).

Geographic Production Shifts. Between 1992 and 2002, world crude steel production increased by 182 million metric tons. During this period, the NAFTA countries' share of global production decreased slightly, from 14.8 percent to 13.6 percent. Over the same period, Japan's strong position weakened somewhat, largely as a result of the persistent weakness of the yen and because reduced demand for Japanese automobiles curtailed Japanese domestic steel consumption. Reduction in capacity by some former central and eastern European countries and the breakup of the Soviet Union repressed production in these areas. This has been offset, however, by increased output in Asian countries other than Japan. Asia now accounts for over 43 percent of world crude steel production, with output from China almost doubling, from 11.2 percent to 20.1 percent (Figure 6).

TABLE 8
THE LARGEST STEEL-PRODUCING COMPANIES, 2002
(MILLION METRIC TONS CRUDE STEEL OUTPUT)

Rank	Company	Steel Output	Rank	Company	Steel Output
1	Arcelor	44.0	6	Corus	16.8
2	LNM Group	34.8	7	Thyssen	16.4
3	Nippon Steel	29.8	8	NKK	15.2
4	POSCO	28.1	9	Riva	15.0
5	Shanghai Baosteel 19.5		10	U.S. Steel	14.4

Source: International Iron and Steel Institute 2003.

Public Policy Lessons from the Steel Industry

1. Neither Subsidy nor Protection Can Roll Back Technological Change and Shifting Comparative Advantage. A recent study has estimated that over the past thirty years, the U.S. steel industry has received subsidies of more than $16 billion, at the same time benefiting from a market strongly protected from foreign competition through the use of antidumping safeguards and countervailing duty actions (Barringer and Pierce 2000). Yet as we have seen, over the same three decades the U.S. steel industry has dramatically shrunk, with employment down by two-thirds and capitalization only one-tenth its former valuation. From 1998 to 2000, the peak years of the dot.com boom, twelve U.S. steel companies filed for bankruptcy (Table 6).

2. The Costs of Steel Protection to the U.S. Economy and U.S. Consumers Far Outweigh the Benefits to the Steel Industry. Even more than with DRAMs and FPDs, the long history of the use of trade remedy laws to protect the steel industry presents a clear example of the costs to the U.S. economy and U.S. consumers far exceeding the benefits to the steel industry. One estimate of the total costs to U.S. consumers over the past three decades places the range between $46 and $76 million in nominal dollars (Barringer and Pierce 2000).

A recent economic study has calculated the effects on the U.S. economy of trade remedy actions that would reduce steel imports by 25 percent (Francois and Baughman 2001). Before recounting these results, it should be recalled that the economic importance of steel-using industries is far greater than that of the steel-producing industry to the overall health of the U.S. economy. Steel-using manufacturers include automobiles and

FIGURE 6
STEEL PRODUCTION: GEOGRAPHICAL DISTRIBUTION,
1992 AND 2002 (IN % OF TOTAL PRODUCTION)

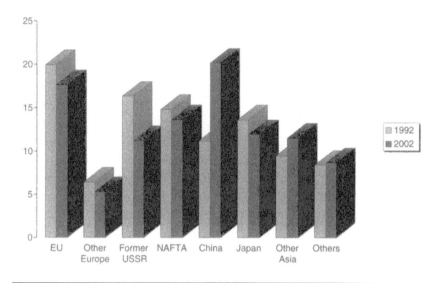

Source: International Iron and Steel Institute 2003.

automobile parts, farm machinery and equipment, construction machinery and equipment, aircraft and parts, electrical equipment, and other fabricated metal products. Depending on how broadly one defines and counts "steel-using" industries, the ratio of steel-using workers to steel-production workers ranges from 20:1 up to 40:1 (Francois and Baughman 2001; Lindsey, Griswold, and Lukas 1999). Steel import protection in effect just transfers money from downstream consuming companies to upstream companies. Prices will rise and be passed on to the ultimate consumer (for example, a domestic car purchaser) for two reasons: less competition from lower-price foreign competitors, and reduced net supply of steel. (Since U.S.-produced steel is not perfectly substitutable with imported steel, a net reduction in supply would occur, and in some cases much higher prices, as the industry would pass the increased price on to manufacturers and consumers.)

Assuming that antidumping duties and safeguard quotas reduce imports by 15 percent, the Francois and Baughman study calculates that the steel industry would benefit by a one-time preservation of some 6,000 jobs; but in return, downstream industries and consumers would be forced to pay about $2.7 billion, or $450,000 per job saved. In addition, given the relative size of the steel and steel-using industries, a rule of thumb would be that for every steel job saved, roughly three steel-using jobs would be jeopardized—in the case in point, about 18,000 jobs.

3. The National Security Defense Remains "the Last Refuge of a Scoundrel," to Paraphrase Dr. Johnson. Inevitably, defenders of steel protection and subsidy have trumpeted the alleged national security implications of downsizing the U.S. steel industry. After 9/11 these pleadings reached a fever pitch, as when a spokesman for the Steelworkers Union stated, "[9/11] should be a reminder to people that steel is a critical industry for the United States, both strategically and economically. Driving steel out of business economically has the same impact as physical bombings" (quoted in Ikenson 2002, 9). This quite recent statement strongly echoes hysterical and false assertions, quoted earlier in this study, by proponents of similar policies for the semiconductor and flat-panel display industries in the 1990s. In what may well be the most misbegotten statement of his presidency, George W. Bush supported this defense connection at an event for the steelworkers, when he stated, "If you're worried about the security of the country and you become over-reliant upon foreign sources of steel, it can easily affect the capacity of our military to be well supplied" (Ikensen 2002, 9).

Fortunately for the president, studies by his own administration belie this dire and foolish assertion. In 2001, the Commerce Department, home of antidumping protection, stated in a study that national defense requirements for finished steel (and by extension iron ore and raw steel) were "very low" and likely to remain so for the foreseeable future. Commerce also stated that domestic demand would "readily be satisfied" by domestic production (U.S. Department of Commerce 2001). Even if these demand projections were not accurate, the huge supply (and oversupply) of steel around the world would assure more than adequate supplies for the Defense Department. As we have seen, more than fifty countries produce steel today in hundreds of plants—hardly a situation that should cause heartburn in the military. The irony is that by cutting off major suppliers of both semifinished and finished steel through the highly protectionist antidumping regime, the United States ultimately hurts its own defense effort—by placing a greater burden on the U.S. economy and U.S. taxpayers to fund legitimate defense needs.

8

Recommendations

Through case studies of the semiconductor, supercomputer, flat-panel-display, and steel industries, this study has attempted to demonstrate both the damage antidumping actions do to market competition and their futility as weapons to save uncompetitive companies and sectors. This is especially the case in high-technology sectors where short product cycles, global strategies and pricing, multiple sourcing of parts, and multinational production facilities render impossible precise targeting of allegedly unfair trade practices. As former Deputy Secretary of the Treasury Ken Dam has warned:

> Potentially even more serious is the impact of antidumping proceedings on the industry structure in many high-tech industries. Modern manufacturing involves use of components. Hence administrative protection through antidumping cases threatens final product manufacturing in the United States (say, in computers as opposed to memory chips). Yet under the applicable law, one cannot take into account the impact on U.S. industries other than the component-making industry. (Dam 2001, 160)

Antidumping actions were problematic in the old economy; they are ludicrous in the new economy.

Further, as some of the most successful U.S. global companies such as IBM, General Motors, and Caterpillar have begun to point out, antidumping actions are two-edged swords that can be wielded against U.S. exporters. Until recently, the United States and the European Union were the leading practitioners of this form of protection. During the 1990s, however, developing countries showed a remarkable learning ability: in 1990, the United States had 193 antidumping orders in place, the EU had 95, and all other countries had 118. By mid-2002, the United States had 264, the EU had 219; and all other countries had 706 (WTO 2002a). In particular, India, South Africa, Mexico, Brazil, and Argentina had become star pupils. As of 2000, more than seventy nations had antidumping laws on their statute books, and each year the number grows (Barfield 1999; Miranda, Torres, and Ruiz 1998; WTO 2002a).

What follows is a series of recommendations for changes in the U.S. antidumping regime and subsequently in WTO trade remedy rules. In recent years, governments, public and private interest groups, and academics have advanced a plethora of reform proposals. Also, as described above, the issue of antidumping reform has emerged as a major point of conflict in the current WTO Doha Round of trade negotiations.

A word about the priorities given to the recommendations: Clearly, the more sweeping the proposed reform, the more difficult it will be to accomplish. Given the overwhelming political power domestic producers have demonstrated over the years, a number of policymakers and policy analysts have drawn back and concentrated on highly technical changes to redress the bias against importers in the extraordinarily complex national and WTO antidumping regimes. This study endorses a number of these proposals, but there are two reasons priority must first be assigned to pressing for more fundamental changes: one, it is important to iterate and reiterate for politicians and the voting public the basic truth that current antidumping regimes are intellectually without foundation and that *even on their own terms* they cannot accomplish intended goals; and two, while many of the technical proposals have real merit, the history of antidumping rules since 1945 demonstrates the ability of domestic producers and their legislative allies quickly to revise and twist proposed technical legislative changes back in a protectionist direction (Finger 1993). Proponents of reform are thus likely to be playing "catch-up" continually.

Repeal Antidumping Laws and Substitute Antitrust Actions

Clearly, if political considerations were not present, the most economically sensible (and equitable) course would be to treat allegations of price discrimination and below-cost pricing as potential infractions against a country's competition policy regime. Under this scenario, domestic antidumping laws would be repealed, and countries would substitute actions against alleged abuses of competition policy or law. Such a course would entail smashing through the rhetorical interpretations of certain historical developments and focusing relentlessly on the underlying economic fundamentals. It would directly challenge arguments made in recent years by both the Clinton and the Bush administrations, which aligned themselves with the flawed and deceptive arguments of academic and legal defenders of antidumping actions.

A prime argument advanced by both the Clinton and Bush administrations is historically accurate but masks an underlying economic falsity: antidumping laws cannot be judged by the same standards as competition policy laws and regulations because they have evolved with different goals in mind and serve different constituencies. As a statement of historical fact, this political divergence is accurate. Taking note of the original common antimonopoly rhetoric of both antitrust and antidumping adherents, Alan Sykes of the University of Chicago has described the evolved and different attributes of the two systems, as follows:

> Antitrust and antidumping law come from the same family tree, but the two branches have diverged widely. . . . [I]n the modern era, antitrust concentrated on the pursuit of economic efficiency . . . address[ing] problems associated with concentrated economic power, primarily through a common law process that left to the courts much of the task of delineating the practices that violate antitrust law. . . . By contrast, antidumping law was intended to create a politically popular form of contingent protection that bears little, if any connection to the prevention of monopoly. . . . Likewise, the political constituency for antidumping law is not an antimonopoly constituency, but one for the protection of industries facing weak markets or long-term decline. (Sykes 1998, 1–2)

Seizing upon this historical divergence, both the Clinton and the Bush administrations have argued that competition policy laws cannot substitute for antidumping laws. As the Clinton administration stated in a brief to a WTO trade and competition policy working group, "If the antidumping laws were eliminated in favor of competition laws or modified to be consistent with competition policy principles, the problems which the antidumping rules seek to remedy would go unaddressed" (WTO 1998, 1).

The fallacy behind this assertion is that all of the antidumping "problems" identified as distinct from competition policy concerns are based upon rationales that cannot stand scrutiny on grounds of either efficiency or equity. Regarding efficiency, Sykes has accurately stated, "Although economic theory identifies a few plausible scenarios in which antidumping measures might enhance economic efficiency, the law remains altogether untailored to identifying them or limiting the use of antidumping measures to plausible cases of efficiency gain" (Sykes 1998, 2). On equity grounds, antidumping actions repeatedly flout a fundamental principle of "fairness" in the multilateral trading system—that is, the principle of national treatment, or that corporations and citizens of foreign countries will receive the same treatment under law that is accorded domestic citizens and corporations. Under antidumping rules, many actions that are clearly legal under U.S. domestic law are deemed "unfair" competition when taken by foreign corporations.

The Underlying Efficiency Principles

As described at the outset of the study, economists have identified a number of circumstances in which dumping, as defined by U.S. and WTO rules (sales below the fully allocated cost of production or international price discrimination) is likely to have no adverse economic consequences. These include "market expansion" dumping, in which a company exports goods at a lower price than it charges in the home market in order to increase worldwide market share; "cyclical dumping," or exporting during periods of low demand and excess production capacity in the home market; "state-trading dumping," in which state-owned entities export at low prices, usually in order to gain hard currency; and "life cycle pricing" in high-tech industries, in which prices are initially set below fully allocated costs in order to generate sales, and over the short life-cycle of the product, "learning by doing" will drastically reduce production costs. As economist Robert Willig has argued, all of these forms of "nonmonopolizing dumping" are "entirely consistent with robustly competitive conditions in the importing nation's market" (Willig 1998, 66).

Predatory ("monopolizing") dumping, however, could very well hurt consumers and producers of the importing nation. Predatory dumping occurs when an exporter has the ability to lower prices for an extended period of time in order to drive companies in the importing country out of business and achieve a monopoly. As we have noted earlier, for predation to be successful, certain market characteristics must apply: a large home market for the exporter; substantial entry and reentry barriers in the exporter's home market and market of the importing nation; relative concentration in the importing market so that monopoly power is readily achieved when a few companies leave the industry; and, if there are several predators, the ability to collude in keeping prices excessively low.

Antitrust authorities, in evaluating anticompetitive effects from alleged predation, could readily contrive a series of rather straightforward questions, such as:

- Is the alleged dumping likely to reduce the number of rivals (both domestic and foreign) in the importing country's market?
- What share of the market would the dumpers have if the complainants left the market?
- Is the market share of the dumpers growing rapidly?
- If there are two or more alleged dumpers, could they plausibly be colluding?
- Are there significant entry and reentry barriers, and concomitantly, does entry require significant capital requirements and sunk costs? (Shin 1998; Willig 1998)

Antitrust authorities in many countries have substantial experience in dealing with just these questions, and there is no reason that such analysis could not be applied in cases of alleged dumping.

Response to "Sanctuary Market" and "Strategic Dumping" Allegations: Target Offending Policies Directly, After Proving That They Exist

If for political reasons, it proves impossible to do away with national antidumping laws entirely, fundamental reforms should be introduced into national antidumping regimes, the aim of which would be to force those systems to address directly and systematically allegations that government policies or market characteristics of the exporting country result in "injurious" dumping into the importing country. (For an analysis with conclusions similar to those set forth here, see Finger and Zlate 2003.)

In recent years, proponents of antidumping actions have advanced a much more sweeping rationale based upon the supposed advantages of firms exporting from so-called "sanctuary markets," or markets that as a result of government policies or private sector practice are closed to outside competitors. This situation need not involve a goal of predation, but it theoretically allows exporters to earn high profits at home and sell abroad at "artificially" low prices. In October 2002, the Bush administration, in a document submitted to the WTO defending current antidumping rules, framed the potential danger this way:

> A government's industrial policies or key aspects of the economic system supported by government inaction can enable injurious dumping to take place. . . . For instance, these policies may allow producers to earn high profits in a home "sanctuary market," which may in turn allow them to sell

abroad at an artificially low price. Such practices can result in injury in the importing country since domestic firms may not be able to match the artificially low prices from producers in the sanctuary market. (WTO 2002b, 4)

The Bush administration's submission is quite brief and a bit sheepish ("antidumping measures should be seen not as an ultimate solution to trade-distorting practices abroad..."). In 1998, however, the Clinton administration had presented a much longer, unabashed defense of the system and a comprehensive review of domestic policies and practices that might trigger antidumping actions. For its candor, *chutzpah*, and the sweeping expansion of the sources of "injurious" dumping, the document deserves careful scrutiny—and rebuttal.

The Clinton administration began by describing a pristine world of "fair" competition based upon "natural" comparative advantage: "In other words, 'fair' trade envisions that producers will use only natural comparative advantages, such as natural resources, a favorable climate, advanced technology, skilled workers, greater efficiency or lower labor costs, and not any artificial advantage." "Injurious" dumping, according to the Clinton submission, results from artificial advantages stemming from two situations: "market-distorting industrial policies and/or differences in national economic systems" (WTO 1998, 7). Antidumping policies, then, constitute a means of achieving a "level playing field."

For the balance of the document, the Clinton administration assembled a veritable farrago of government policies and "differences in national economic systems" that, in its view, lead to injurious dumping. Included in this list is an extraordinarily diverse set of examples, including: high tariffs; government subsidies; price controls; government limitations on investment; limitations on the number of producers in a particular sector; anticompetitive sanitary and phytosanitary standards; a range of services barriers, including restrictions of provision of financial services, regulation of international data flows and data processing; misuse of standards, testing and certification procedures; permissive policies toward vertical and horizontal restraints of competition; cross-subsidization in multiproduct firms; employment and social policies that result in "artificial" advantages for domestic firms; and contrasting business practices that give rise to differing debt/equity structures between domestic and foreign firms.

The above list is not complete, but the inescapable conclusion is that virtually every area of domestic public policy can be a cause of antidumping action under this expansive interpretation of artificial advantages.

This study will comment on only a selected few of the examples advanced in the submission.

Market-Distorting Industrial Policies. It should be noted that the line between public policies and differences in economic systems is blurred, and so the following designations are somewhat arbitrary. High tariffs and subsidies are two of the simplest government (industrial) policies to describe and rebut as necessitating the use of antidumping actions. The tariff rates have been set as a result of negotiations by individual nations in the Uruguay Trade Round. If a nation has negotiated high tariffs, so be it; if it breaks the agreement and raises its rates, it must renegotiate rates with all other members of the WTO or face retaliation. Industrial subsidies lead to a similar situation: the WTO has set rules for illegal and legal subsidies, and if a nation believes these rules have been violated, it will bring a case to the WTO—thus obviating (indeed precluding) the use of national trade remedy systems.

The submission also mentions government policies to limit the number of producers in a sector or limitations on foreign equity participation or ownership in a sector. Two points are relevant in this case: First, like other nations, the United States has long limited investment in certain quite important sectors, such as airlines and telecommunications. It thus comes with ill grace for the U.S. government to take unilateral action against other governments for the same practice. Second, GATT and WTO rules, except in unusual circumstances generally in the services area, do not cover investment issues; thus, there are no legal impediments to governments' applying certain restrictions (as the United States has done).

The examples cited relating to rules for competition are also of questionable validity, particularly with regard to cross-subsidization and relaxed limitations on vertical restraints.

In the United States and numerous other countries, many firms have multiple product lines, and there is no restriction on cross-subsidization *per se*, absent some other anticompetitive practice by the firms. Thus, companies such as IBM and Texas Instruments for many years produced computers and computer components such as chips, with chips being priced to increase the competitiveness of the final product. In no case did the U.S. government object—nor should it have. Similarly, while U.S. competition policy has changed greatly over the past half-century, current thinking holds that under most conditions vertical restraints of trade are not anticompetitive. To lump these industry practices as evidence of an "artificial" advantage is hypocritical and deceptive.

Differences in National Economies. Several of the above citations could also be counted as the result of "differences in national economies." But the most significant example given by the Clinton administration is the potential for "injurious dumping . . . when social and legal arrangements for employment and under-employment differ between countries. . . ." The Clinton submission (odd for an administration with at least vaguely social democratic aspirations) in effect charges that industries in nations with greater protection of labor and employment will unfairly reduce prices while forced to hold onto existing employees during economic downturns. Under this proposed reading of antidumping laws, most nations of the European Union, whose domestic laws contain many such protections for labor organizations and employment, would seem to face the prospect of endless antidumping actions.

With the introduction of potential injurious dumping from national labor practices or social welfare systems, the questions raised by the current rationale for dumping actions have moved far from border prices and deep into the social and economic fabric of individual nations. Under current antidumping regimes in any country, judgments cannot be established about whether a nation's labor practices, allegedly lax rules on vertical integration, subsidies to key industries, or health and safety regulations create artificial advantages or are merely evidence of "robustly competitive" conditions in importing markets.

Reform of U.S. (and WTO) Antidumping Rules

By broadening the alleged goals of antidumping laws to include a defense against all "artificial" or "unnatural" advantages, defenders of the current system have opened a Pandora's box for themselves. Even the most ardent proponents admit that the mere existence of price discrimination or below-cost sales does not "prove" market distortions in the exporting economy are the causal factor. Many perfectly natural competitive conditions can cause variations in price. To be credible and fair, therefore, U.S. rules and the WTO Antidumping Agreement should mandate that the petitioning industry and the domestic antidumping authority identify the purported market distortion and establish a causal connection between this alleged distortion and injurious dumping, as evidence by either below-cost sales or price discrimination. If, for instance, government limitation on the number of producers in a sector results in a closed sanctuary market that allows below-cost pricing in foreign markets, that competitive impediment should be identified and the injurious connection established. Similarly, if cross-subsidization in multiproduct companies results in component prices that have no relation to costs of production, this subsidization should be pointed out and made part of any antidumping allegation. The respondents should be given the opportunity to rebut, with evidence to the contrary, all allegations regarding market-distorting government policies or "differences in economic systems" that result in "unnatural" advantages.

As envisioned here, the presentations of the petitioner and the respondent would largely establish the facts and economic evidence in a case, though the government agency should be allowed limited investigatory power to clear up conflicting claims by the two private parties. This compromise—regarding the roles of the private parties and the government agency in the importing country—attempts to balance a concern that national antidumping authorities will create huge new factual burdens on the foreign respondents against the reality that, given the expanded causal connections that must be established, these antidumping authorities may need some independent analysis and counsel.

Competition Policy Analysis. In addition, certain elements of the antitrust economic analysis should be introduced into antidumping proceedings. First, a clear distinction should be drawn between industries with a large number of producers worldwide and those with relatively few producers. By and large, the presumption would be that dumping cannot occur when many firms are competing against one another in numerous markets. (An exception would be if the importing country could demonstrate the existence of a cartel fixing domestic prices in the exporting country, or the existence of an international cartel.) Under this scenario, a high legal threshold would exist for proof of dumping in the steel industry as it has evolved worldwide.

In industries where there are only a few producers and the possibility of sanctuary markets exists, the priority of the WTO should be opening the sanctuary market of the exporting country, not creating another sanctuary market in the importing country. Antidumping authorities that claim sustained differential-price dumping should be required to produce an explanation of how a higher price is maintained in the home market, either through private action or with some government support. Once they satisfactorily provide this explanation, negotiations would first be conducted between the exporting-country and importing-country governments, aimed at dismantling the barriers to entry into the sanctuary market. Should these fail, antidumping penalties could be imposed immediately. Evidence from these negotiations could also be grounds for antidumping actions by other WTO members (Hindley and Messerlin 1996).

The National Interest. A third reform is the expansion of antidumping economic analysis to include an assessment of the costs and benefits of individual actions across the entire economy. Presently, only the costs to the petitioning industry are examined by the USITC. A broader analysis, as suggested here, would include the costs and benefits to corporate users of the dumped products, as well as the overall costs to final consumers of the product. As noted above, consumer groups and downstream corporate industries should have standing to appear before antidumping authorities to present evidence and their viewpoints into the proceedings. In the current Doha Round, the European Union, as well as a group of nations pushing for substantial reforms in the WTO antidumping regime, have endorsed the idea of a "public interest test" to measure the effects of antidumping orders on the whole national economy, not just on the fortunes of the petitioning industry (*ITR* May 2, 2002; July 11, 2002).

In the longer term, policymakers should give serious consideration to a more fundamental structural change in the U.S. antidumping regime: providing that in certain circumstances, the president can intervene at the end of the process, invoke a national interest clause, and craft a solution that is based upon economic considerations in combination with other U.S. national political goals and imperatives. The original reason behind granting authority to an independent commission (USITC) on antidumping cases was to ensure a nonpolitical, "scientific" decision. However, the history of the current process for deciding antidumping cases renders laughable the idea that science or fundamental economic theory plays any significant part in the final antidumping determinations. There are two reasons for this: one, over the past four decades, Congress has continuously legislated rules and instructions to the USITC which overwhelmingly tilt the criteria for "injurious" dumping in favor of the domestic petitioners; and two, with some outstanding exceptions, members of the commission have been political hacks, with neither interest in nor competence for economic analysis. More often than not, they are congressional staffers who use the position as a stepping stone to lucrative private sector jobs or more prestigious executive branch appointments.

More broadly, a body of literature and analysis now exists that questions independent commissions in general (see Wallison 2003). Those who argue against allowing the president or his direct appointees to have a say in the final determination claim the process would be subject to great political influence and lobbying. The argument on the other side—particularly given the evolution of the antidumping regime—is that capture of an independent commission by the regulated industry, either through legislative fiat or control of appointments, means that the public interest has already been subverted, and in this circumstance would be better served by a direct and transparent judgment by a political officer. Also, in the trade remedy area, safeguard actions end with a final political decision by the president, as discussed below. With all the political pressures that have come to bear on this process over the years, the outcomes on safeguards dictated by the White House have generally served the national interest well.

Substitute Safeguard Actions for Antidumping

The final broad, longer-range recommendation is to shift national trade remedy actions away from antidumping toward the greater use of safeguard actions. Under U.S. law (Section 201 of the basic trade law), as sanctioned by WTO rules, the government may intervene to ameliorate the negative effect of import surges on industries and workers. As Section 201 operates—upon petition by an industry or union, the House and Senate trade committees, or the president—the USITC may determine an industry is threatened by "serious" injury caused by a sudden increase in imports and recommend remedies to the president, who then makes the final decision. Under current WTO rules, the relief can be granted for up to four years, with the possibility of an extension for another four years. (If the relief is granted for less than three years, other countries cannot demand compensation for tariff increases or quantitative restrictions that are part of the remedy.)

There are four strong advantages for substituting safeguard actions for antidumping actions (Barfield 1999). First, safeguard actions are much more flexible in both substance and duration; the president, who has final authority to put the trade remedy package together, can tailor such a package to match individual situations. As we have seen, antidumping duties, once levied, remain in place for at least five years—and thus can continue long after the alleged dumping has ended.

Second, in determining a safeguard action, the president can take into account the overall national welfare (including consumer and corporate users' interests) and other political and diplomatic factors—which cannot be done with antidumping. For example, in the semiconductor and flat-panel displays situations of the late 1980s, use of safeguards would have allowed the Reagan and Bush administrations to assess the overall impact of trade actions on the U.S. computer industry.

Third, safeguard actions require that the petitioning industry, as a condition of receiving temporary protection, put together a plan to increase its competitiveness. Thus, unlike antidumping actions, safeguards introduce pressure for action-forcing results and do not allow industries to drift supinely for years under the cover of government protection (though in many cases a successful recovery strategy may not be possible).

Finally, increased use of safeguard actions would reduce the inflammatory and often-spurious comparisons made between "fair" and "unfair" trade practices. With more naked honesty, the government would temporarily decrease imports in order to allow a U.S. industry to put together and execute a plan for recovery. Certainly there would be pressure to extend these bailouts to the fullest allowable time, but at least consumers and U.S. industries whose interests would be damaged by the protective package could have their voices heard in opposition up front and on a continuing basis.[5]

Important Technical Changes to Antidumping Rules

During 2002, a group of WTO members opposed to current WTO rules governing antidumping actions put forward several sets of proposals for major technical changes relating to procedures, methods of calculation for antidumping duties, and the means of determining injury to a domestic industry. Among the nations who have signed on to these proposals (the group is loosely called the "Friends of Antidumping") are: Brazil, Chile, Colombia, Costa Rica, Hong Kong, Israel, Japan, Mexico, Norway, Singapore, South Korea, Switzerland, Thailand, and Turkey (*ITR* May 2, 2002; July 11, 2002; November 28, 2002). Scholars at the Cato Institute have published several excellent studies detailing the flaws in the current rules and offering analytically strong analysis and twenty-one recommendations for reform (Lindsey and Ikenson 2002a, 2002b). In December 2002, the United States signaled its strong opposition to many of the proposals of the "Friends of Antidumping." The EU, in typical fashion, is trying to have it both ways—on the one hand courting proponents of reform by backing a few of their recommendations, while on the other hand opposing key elements of the reform package, which would force substantial changes in the current EU antidumping regime.

Full details of all of the proposed technical reforms are available in the Lindsey and Ikenson trade policy papers and on the WTO website. For this study, only the most important recommendations will be described and endorsed.

Revise Existing Rules for Cost Comparisons Between Home and Foreign Market Sales. Under current WTO rules (Article 2.2.1 of the Antidumping Agreement), dumping margins are determined by a comparison of export prices to "normal" prices in the exporter's home market. The problem lies in the determination of which prices are "normal" and stem from the "ordinary course of trade." Under the cost test now allowed, antidumping authorities may exclude home market prices that are found to be below the cost of production. This produces comparisons of all export prices with prices in the home market that are above the cost of production (that is, with the highest prices). Such an asymmetric method of calculation and comparison inevitably skews the result toward a finding of dumping, and Lindsey and Ikenson call it the "most egregious methodological distortion in contemporary antidumping practice." They go on to point out, "The existence of below-cost sales in the home market is actually affirmative evidence of the *absence* of a sanctuary market. A sanctuary market, after all, is supposed to be an island of artificially high prices and profits. If home-market sales at a loss are found in significant quantities, isn't that a fairly compelling indication that there is no sanctuary market?" (Lindsey and Ikenson 2002b, 15).

Reformers call for Article 2.2.1 to be rewritten to clarify that under most circumstances, sales below the cost of production should not be excluded automatically. Only under specific circumstances—for example, sales of damaged goods—should these exclusions be allowed.

Zeroing. Under this practice, in determining dumping margins, national authorities use different methodologies to compare export producer prices with the "normal value" of prices in the importing country (usually determined by the average price of like products in the home market). When the export price is lower than the normal value in the importing market, the difference becomes the basis for the amount of dumping for that sale. However, when the export price is higher than the normal value in the importing market, the dumping amount is calculated as zero. The results are then averaged to arrive at a dumping margin, which is then assessed as the final dumping duty. Obviously, zeroing out lower-than-average prices for exporters skews the result toward a conclusion that dumping has occurred, even when it clearly has not.

In March 2001, the WTO's Appellate Body ruled that the EU's application of "zeroing" violated WTO rules, concluding that it did not meet the standards of articles 2.4 and 2.4.2 of the Antidumping Agreement, which required a "fair comparison" between export price and normal values. Without taking into account the prices of *all* comparable export transactions, the EU's application could not provide a "fair comparison" (WTO 2001a). However, the extent to which this ruling will force widespread changes in price comparisons remains uncertain. On technical grounds not dealt with here, the EU has only partially complied, and the U.S. Department of Commerce has not changed its zeroing practices, even though they would seem clearly to go against the Appellate Body's decision.

In order to give full force to the sensible and equitable conclusion of the Appellate Body, current Doha Round antidumping negotiations should amend Article 2 of the WTO Antidumping Agreement to prohibit zeroing at any point in antidumping proceedings. Thus, in the determination of antidumping margins, when export prices are higher than normal value they should be given their exact value when averaged in with other export prices.

"Lesser Duty" Application. Article 9.1 of the Antidumping Agreement encourages WTO members to establish dumping duties only to the level that will remove the injury to the domestic industry: specifically, it states it is "desirable" that antidumping duties "be less than the [dumping] margin if such lesser duty would be adequate to remove the injury to the domestic industry." The EU and some other WTO members follow this practice and apply a "lesser duty rule" when determining dumping duties. Research has shown a substantial difference in some cases between the final dumping margins and the actual rate that would be noninjurious. Since the avowed aim of the antidumping action is to remove injury, the Article 9.1 provision should be amended to require that antidumping duties be less than the dumping margin, if the lesser duty is sufficient to remove the injury.

Causation of Injury. The current system of rules for determining whether foreign dumping has injured a domestic industry is flawed and unworkable. In addition to establishing that dumping has occurred, the WTO Antidumping Agreement requires a finding that dumped imports are causing or threatening to cause "material injury" to the affected industry, before dumping remedies can be applied. Unfortunately, the agreement does not provide standards or a methodology for determining a causal connection between dumping and material injury of the domestic industry.

In the United States and a number of other WTO member countries, the standard used by the antidumping authorities merely seeks to establish dumping as "a cause" of the injury. This allows the U.S. Department of Commerce to ignore the impact of overall economic conditions, the competitive condition of the industry, and a host of other factors that could be the real cause of lower export prices and increased imports.

The Uruguay Round made an attempt to tighten up the criteria for finding "material injury" as a result of dumping. Specifically, Article 3.5 of the Antidumping Agreement provides that dumping authorities are required "to examine any known factors other than dumped imports which at the same time are injuring the domestic industry, and the injuries caused by these other factors must not be attributed to the dumped imports" (WTO 1995). In a 2001 case, the Appellate Body of the WTO, in interpreting the new mandate, muddied the water by introducing what even opponents of antidumping regimes admit is probably an impossible standard for determining injury. The Appellate Body ruled that antidumping authorities identify all the factors that could be causing injury, disentangle them from the effects of alleged dumping, and calculate the injurious impacts separately, though it admitted that, as a practical matter, it might not be easy to distinguish the specific effects of different causal factors (WTO 2001b). Defenders of antidumping regimes argue that if this ruling becomes the new standard, demonstrating injury will be virtually impossible. Even opponents of most antidumping practices and rules fear a backlash that could result in much laxer injury standards.

In order to avoid this result, the Doha Round antidumping negotiations should take up the issue and reach agreement on a new standard. The focus should be to isolate the effects of alleged dumping and draw back from the enormously complicated and analytically difficult goal of evaluating and putting a number on all possible causes of injury to the domestic industry. If dumping alone is found to be a substantial cause, or even a threat, of material injury, then injury is established and duties can be levied.

Afterword

A decade ago, Michael Finger, one of the most astute analysts of antidumping laws and practices, stated simply, "Antidumping is ordinary protection with a grand public relations program" (Finger 1993, 34). In tracing the damaging and counterproductive outcomes of U.S. antidumping policy in four high-technology sectors, this study has demonstrated the continuing validity of Finger's observation. But while economists and other trade policy wonks (like the author) will continue to hammer away at the irrationality of antidumping, the best hope for reform of the system lies in the fact that protectionist chickens (that is, antidumping actions) are coming home to roost—and increasingly U.S. exporting firms and sectors are finding themselves the object of the same arbitrary findings that have plagued imports to the U.S. market. We can only hope, over the next few years, that a combination of exporting U.S. firms and users of higher-priced "dumped" imported products will join forces to change the political calculus in Congress and the electorate.

Notes

1. Some portions of this study, now updated, originally appeared in Claude E. Barfield and Mark A. Groombridge, "The Irrationality of Anti-Dumping Laws in the New Economy," *International Studies Review* 3, no. 2 (December 2000): 1–29.

2. On September 14, 2003, just as this study was going to press, the WTO Ministerial Meeting to chart a course for the conclusion of the Doha Round in 2004 collapsed in disagreement. At this point, it is almost certain that the deadline for the conclusion of the round by the end of 2004 will not be met; and negotiations will go on until the end of 2006. This new deadline stems from the fact Congress has granted expedited clearance of trade agreements (so-called fast-track authority) only until the end of 2006.

At the ministerial meeting in Cancun Mexico, antidumping issues did not play a prominent role; the reason is that the language of the original Doha Declaration (infra 7), even with the conflicting interpretations, fixed the parameters of future Doha Round negotiations. There are many media accounts of the history and fate of the Cancun ministerial meeting; for detailed analyses, see ITR September 4, 11, 18, 2003. For an article assigning responsibility among the WTO members and coalitions, see Barfield and Glassman 2003.

3. With vector processors, memory is "shared": only one instruction is needed to perform an operation on an array of numbers. Non-vector systems, or parallel processing, require as many instructions as there are numbers.

4. As this study was going to press, the Bush administration was conducting a mid-course review of the original safeguard actions, in order to determine whether these protectionist actions should be partially and wholly ended, or remain in place. For an analysis of the conflicting pressures and arguments relating to the current steel safeguards, see Stone 2003. For a discussion of the implications of the Bush administration steel safeguard actions in relation to policy recommendations made in this study, see note 5.

5. While this study is not the place to present a detailed analysis of the ongoing debate over the president's decision to impose safeguard actions for many steel products in March 2002, several points should be noted that are relevant to the above recommendations. First, evidence of the greater substantive and political flexibility in the Section 201 process abounds in the unfolding of events. The USITC did undertake a midterm review of the economic impact of the 2002 steel

safeguards on the U.S. economy and published its finding on September 19, 2003 (USITC 2003a, 2003b). Though its findings were controversial and disputed by all sides (USITC did not find significant positive or negative impacts on the total U.S. economy), the report did trigger an important public debate that set forth the pros and cons of the steel safeguard actions. This political—and public—debate will continue as the Bush White House decides whether or not to continue the safeguards protection, curtail it, or eliminate it altogether this fall. Second, the process has produced a new phenomenon in the emergence of a strong counterforce to steel producers and workers—that is, a coalition of industry steel users (Consuming Industries Trade Action Coalition) and consumer organizations (Consumers for World Trade and others) who have mounted a strong campaign to scrap the safeguards. Such a political process and debate is not possible under more restrictive and closed rules for antidumping proceedings. The president may well decide to favor the steel industry for political (as well as substantive) reasons; but the decision process, and the political jockeying that has accompanied it, has been fully and comprehensively reported in the press. For analysis of the current political debate, see Stone 2003 and Allen and Weisman 2003. For analysis of the substantive pros and cons of the safeguard actions, see ITR March 27, August 14, 2003; Lawrence 2003; and Hogan and Hartson 2003.

References

Acs, Zolton J. 1984. *The Changing Structure of the U.S. Economy: Lessons from the Steel Industry.* New York: Praeger.

Allen, Mike and Jonathan Weisman. 2003. Steel Tariffs Appear to Backfire. *Washington Post.* September 19.

American Iron and Steel Institute. 2003. http://www.steel.org.

Anchordoguy, Marie. 1994. Japanese-American Trade Conflict and Supercomputers. *Political Science Quarterly* 109 (1): 35-80.

Association of Iron and Steel Engineers (AISE). 2003. *Steel News.* https://www.steelnews.com/companies/steel_bankruptcies.htm.

Barfield, Claude. 1994. Flat-Panel Displays: A Second Look. *Issues in Science and Technology.* Fall: 27–32.

————. 1995. Flat-Panel Initiative: A Bad Idea. *Issues in Science and Technology.* Summer: 9–10.

————. 1999. Safeguards vs. Antidumping Protection: Lessons from the Steel "Crisis." *On the Issues.* Washington, D.C.: American Enterprise Institute, June.

————. 2002. Nerves of Steel. *Financial Times.* March 1.

Barfield, Claude and James K. Glassman. 2003. The Real Cancun: What Went Wrong at the Trade Talks. *The Weekly Standard.* October 6, 15–16.

Barfield, Claude and Mark A. Groombridge. 2000. The Irrationality of Anti-Dumping Laws in the New Economy. *International Studies Review.* Vol. 3, No. 2, December.

Barnett, Donald F. and Robert W. Crandall. 1986. *Up From the Ashes: The Rise of the Steel Minimills in the United States.* Washington, D.C.: The Brookings Institution.

Barnett, Donald F. and Louis Schorsch. 1983. *Steel: Upheaval in a Basic Industry.* Cambridge, Mass.: Ballinger Publishing Company.

Barringer, William and Kenneth J. Pierce. 2000. *Paying the Price for Big Steel: $100 Billion in Trade Restraints and Corporate Welfare.* Washington, D.C.: American Institute for International Steel.

Boltuck, Richard and Robert E. Litan, eds. 1991. *Down in the Dumps: Administration of the Unfair Trade Laws.* Washington, D.C.: The Brookings Institution.

Boskin, Michael and Lawrence J. Lau. 1996. Contributions of R&D to Economic Growth. In Bruce L.R. Smith and Claude E. Barfield, eds. *Technology, R&D,*

and the Economy. Washington, D.C.: The Brookings Institution and the American Enterprise Institute.

Cooney, Stephen. 2003. Semiconductors: the High-Technology Downturn and Issues in the 108th Congress. *CRS Report for Congress* No. RL 31708. Washington, D.C.: U.S. Library of Congress, January 22.

Council of Economic Advisors. 2001. *The Economic Report of the President, 2001*. Washington, D.C.: Government Printing Office, January.

———. 2003. *The Economic Report of the President, 2003*. Washington, D.C.: Government Printing Office, February.

Council on Competitiveness. 1993. *Road Map for Results: Trade Policy, Technology and American Competitiveness: Case Studies*. Washington, D.C.

Crandall, Robert W. 1981. *The U.S. Steel Industry in Recurrent Crisis*. Washington, D.C.: The Brookings Institution.

Dam, Kenneth W. 2001. *The Rules of the Global Game: A New Look at International Economic Policymaking*. Chicago: University of Chicago Press.

Dataquest. 2002. Semiconductor Industry Worldwide. Report, online database. http://www3.gartner.com/pages/story.php.id.2097.s.8.jsp (accessed November 20, 2002).

Dick, Andrew. 1995. *Missing the Target: Industrial Policy and Semiconductors*. Washington, D.C.: American Enterprise Institute.

Dumler, Christopher M. 1997. Antidumping Laws Trash Supercomputer Computer. *Trade Policy Briefing* No. 32. Washington, D.C.: The Cato Institute, October 14.

Durling, James P. of Willkie Farr & Gallagher LLP. 2002. Interview by the author. December.

Ernst and Young Consulting. 1989. *Report on Government Assistance to the U.S. Steel Industry*. Mimeo: Ernst and Young Consulting, October.

Financial Times, various issues.

Finger, J. Michael. 1993. *Antidumping: How It Works and Who Gets Hurt*. Ann Arbor: University of Michigan Press.

Finger, J. Michael and Andrei Zlate. 2003. WTO Rules Allow New Trade Restrictions: The Public Interest is a Bastard Child. Paper Prepared for the U.N. Millennium Project Task Force on Trade. Washington, D.C.: April.

Flamm, Kenneth. 1994. Flat-Panel Displays: Catalyzing a U.S. Industry. *Issues in Science and Technology*. Fall: 27–32.

———. 1995. In Defense of the Flat-Panel Initiative. *Issues in Science and Technology*. Spring: 22–25.

———. 1996. *Mismanaged Trade: Strategic Trade Policy and the Semiconductor Industry*. Washington, D.C.: The Brookings Institution.

Francois, Joseph F. and Laura M. Baughman. 2001. Costs to American Consuming Industries of Steel Quotas and Taxes. Washington D.C.: The Citac Foundation, April 30.

Goldman, T. R. 1996. Computer War Illuminates Free Trade Politics. *American Law Media: The Recorder.* August 5.

Griswold, Daniel T. 1999. Counting the Cost of Steel Protection. Washington, D.C.: The Cato Institute, February 25.

Harbrecht, Douglas, Paul Magnusson, and Gary McWilliams. 1993. Did Commerce Pull the Plug on Flat-Screen Makers? *Business Week.* July 5.

Hart, Jeffrey. 1993. The Antidumping Petition of the Advanced Display Manufacturers of America: Origins and Consequences. *World Economy* 16: 85–109.

Hindley, Brian and Patrick A. Messerlin. 1996. *Antidumping Industrial Policy.* Washington, D.C.: American Enterprise Institute.

Hoerr, John P. 1988. *And the Wolf Finally Came: The Decline of the American Steel Industry.* Pittsburgh: University of Pittsburgh Press.

Hogan, William T. 1994. *Steel in the 21st Century: Competition Forges a New World Order.* Lexington, Mass.: Lexington Books.

Hogan and Hartson LLP International Trade Group. 2003. The Steel Decision and Its Consequences. Presentation April 18, 2002. Washington, D.C.

Hufbauer, Gary Clyde and Ben Goodrich. 2001. Steel: Big Problems, Better Solutions. *International Economic Policy Brief* No. PBO1-9. Washington D.C.: Institute for International Economics, July.

———. 2002. Time for a Grand Bargain in Steel. *International Economic Policy Brief* No. PBO2-1. Washington, D.C.: Institute for International Economics, January.

Ikenson, Dan. 2001. Antidumping Laws Hurt American Consumers. *CTPS Articles.* March 7.

———. 2002. Steel Trap: How Subsidies and Protection Weaken the U.S. Steel Industry. *Briefing Paper* No. 14. Washington, D.C.: The Cato Institute, March 1.

Industry Trade Reports. 1997–2000. *Cahner's Instat Group, De Dios & Associates, IC Insights, Integrated Circuit Engineering and Dataquest.*

Infineon Technology. 2002. *Worldwide Locations.* http://www.infineon.com/comp/worldwide/ww_locations.htm

Inside U.S. Trade. August 2, 1996.

———. May 24, 1996.

International Iron and Steel Institute (IISI). 2003. *World Steel in Figures.* http://www.worldsteel.org/media/wsif/wsif2003.pdf.

International Trade Reporter, various issues.

Irwin, Douglas A. 1996. Trade Politics and the Semiconductor Industry. In Anne O. Krueger, ed. *The Political Economy of American Trade Policy.* Chicago: University of Chicago Press.

———. 1998. The Semiconductor Industry. In Robert Z. Lawrence, ed. *Brookings Trade Forum: 1998.* Washington, D.C.: The Brookings Institution.

Japan Economic Institute. 1993. *Japan Economic Report* No. 3B. Washington, D.C.: Japan Economic Institute, January 29.

Johnson, Brian T. 1992. A Guide to Antidumping Laws: America's Unfair Trade Practice. *Background* No. 9-6, Washington, D.C.: The Heritage Foundation, July 21.

Johnson, Chalmers. 1995. *Japan, Who Governs?* New York: W. W. Norton & Company.

Journal of Commerce. 1997. Editorial Opinion: Free Foreign Supercomputers. *Journal of Commerce.* September 3.

Judis, John B. 1993. Flat-Panel Flop: How Not to Conduct Trade Policy. *New Republic.* August 9.

Lawrence, Robert Z., ed. 1998. *Brookings Trade Forum: 1998.* Washington, D.C.: The Brookings Institution.

———. 2003. Bush Had the Right to Impose Tariffs on Steel. *Financial Times,* January 29.

Lindsey, Brink. 1992. The DRAM Scam. *Reason.* February.

———. 1999. The U.S. Antidumping Law: Rhetoric versus Reality. *Trade Policy Briefing* No. 7. Washington, D.C.: The Cato Institute, August 16.

Lindsey, Brink, Daniel T. Griswold, and Aaron Lukas. 1999. The Steel "Crisis" and the Costs of Protection. *Trade Briefing Paper* No. 4. Washington, D.C.: The Cato Institute, April 16.

Lindsey, Brink and Dan Ikenson. 2001. Coming Home to Roost: Proliferating Antidumping Laws and the Growing Threat to U.S. Exports. *Trade Policy Analysis* No. 14. Washington, D.C.: The Cato Institute, July 30.

———. 2002a. Antidumping 101: The Devilish Details of "Unfair Trade" Law. *Briefing Paper* No. 20. Washington, D.C.: The Cato Institute, November 26.

———. 2002b. Reforming the Antidumping Agreement: A Road Map for WTO Negotiations. *Briefing Paper* No. 21. Washington, D.C.: The Cato Institute, December 11.

Litan, Robert E. and Richard D. Boltuck, eds. 1991. *Administration of the Trade Remedy Laws.* Washington, D.C.: The Brookings Institution.

Magee, Robert W. and Yeomin Yoon. 1994. Trade Policy in the Computer Industry: Time for a Change. *Temple International and Comparative Law Journal* 8: 219–258.

Maggs, John. 1996. Cray to File Trade Complaint Against Leading Competitor. *Journal of Commerce.* July 30.

———. 1997. Cray Wins "Vector" Fight, Sort Of. *Journal of Commerce.* September 29.

Manyin, Mark E., Stephen Cooney, and Jeanne J. Grimmett. 2002. The Semiconductor Industry and South Korea's Hynix Corporation. *CRS Report for Congress* RL 31238. Washington, D.C.: The Library of Congress, updated January 21, 2003.

Maur, Jean-Christophe and Patrick A. Messerlin. 1999. Antidumping in Supercomputers or Supercomputing in Antidumping? The Cray-NEC Case. Mimeo.

Messerlin, Patrick A. and Yoshiyuki Noguchi. 1998. Antidumping Policies in Electronic Products. In Robert Z. Lawrence, ed. *Brookings Trade Forum: Part One, Antidumping*. Washington, D.C.: The Brookings Institution.

Miranda, Jorge, Raul A. Torres, and Mario Ruiz. 1998. The International Use of Antidumping: 1987–1997. *Journal of World Trade* 32: 5–71.

Monterey Institute. 2001. International Commercial Diplomacy Project. *Case Studies: Trade and Investment Strategies in the Flat Panel Display Industry (1968–1998)*. http://www.commercialdiplomacy.org/case_flatpanel.htm.

Nec Corp vs. United States. 151 F. 3rd 1361, 12376 (Fed. Cir., 1998).

Prestowitz, Clyde V. Jr. 1989. *Trading Places*. New York: Basic Books, Inc.

Reid, T.R. 1991. The Commerce Department's Bonehead Play. *Washington Post National Weekly Edition*. September 23–29.

Robertson, Jack. 1998. Micron: Acquiring a More Global Reach. *Electronic Business News*. October 14.

Samsung Electronics. 2002. *Timeline and History*. http://www.samsungelectronics.com/company/division/semiconductors/history.htm.

Sanger, David E. 1991. U.S. Tariff Appears to Backfire. *New York Times*. September 26.

Scherer, Frederick M. 1992. *International High-Technology Competition*. Cambridge, Mass.: Harvard University Press.

Schneider, Greg. 2003. Big Steel on the Rebound: Consolidation Leaves Workers, Retirees Shouldering Benefit Cuts. *Washington Post*. February 18.

Shin, Hyun Ja. 1998. Possible Instances of Predatory Pricing in Recent U.S. Antidumping Cases. In Robert Z. Lawrence, ed. *Brookings Trade Forum: 1998*. Washington, D.C.: The Brookings Institution.

Sorkin, Andrew Ross. 2003. A Contrarian Bets That Steel Has A Future. *New York Times*. January 7.

Steel Manufacturers Association. 2003a. Growth of U.S. Minimill Industry, 1970–2003. http://www.steelnet.org/archive/WIIT_110201_files/frame.htm.

———. 2003b. Statement of Thomas A. Danjczek Before Members of the House Steel Caucus, September 25. http://www.steelnet.org/new/20030925.htm.

Stone, Peter H. 2003. Turmoil over Tariffs. *National Journal*. October 4, 3048–3049.

Sykes, Alan O. 1998. Antidumping and Antitrust: What Problems Does Each Address? In Robert Z. Lawrence, ed. *Brookings Trade Forum: 1998*. Washington, D.C.: The Brookings Institution.

Tiffany, Paul A. 1988. *The Decline of American Steel: How Management, Labor and Government Went Wrong*. New York: Oxford University Press.

Tornell, Aaron. 1997. Rational Atrophy: The U.S. Steel Industry. *Working Paper No. 6084*. Cambridge, Mass.: National Bureau of Economic Research, July.

Tyson, Laura D'Andrea and David B. Yoffie. 1993. Semiconductors: From Manipulated to Managed Trade. In David B. Yoffie, ed. *Beyond Free Trade*. Cambridge, Mass.: Harvard Business School Press.

U.S. Bureau of Labor Statistics. 2002. Chapter on Steel Manufacturing (SIC 331). *Occupational Outlook Handbook 2000–2001*. Washington, D.C.

U.S. Census Bureau. 2003. U.S. Domestic Steel Shipments and Import Percentage of Apparent Domestic Consumption, 1992–2002. http://www.census.gov/cir/www/331/m331j.htm.

U.S. Department of Commerce. 1995. *Micron Technology v. United States*. 893 F. Supp. 21, Court of International Trade.

———. 1996. *Dynamic Random Access Memory Semiconductors of One Megabit and Above from the Republic of Korea*. 61 Federal Register 4765-55, February 8.

———. 1999. *Anti-dumping Duty on Dynamic Random Access Memory Semi-conductors of One Megabit and Above from the Republic of Korea*. Report of Panel, WT/DS99/R. January 29. http://www.wto.org.

———. 2000. *Final Results of Full Sunset Review and Revocation of Order, DRAMs from Korea*. 65 Fed. Reg. 59391. October 5.

———. Bureau of Export Administration. 2001. *The Effects of Imports of Iron Ore and Semi-Finished Steel on National Security*. An investigation conducted under Section 232 of the Trade Expansion Act of 1962, as amended October 2001.

U.S. Department of Defense. 1987. *Defense Semiconductor Dependency*. Washington, D.C.: Defense Science Task Force, February.

U.S. Government, Executive Office of the President. 1972. *Report of the President's Advisory Committee on Executive Organization*. Washington, D.C.: Government Printing Office.

U.S. International Trade Commission. 1993. *Dynamic Random Access Memory Semiconductors of One Megabit and Above from the Republic of Korea*. Pub. 2629. May.

———. 1999a. *Dynamic Random Access Memory Semiconductors of One Megabit and Above from Taiwan*. Pub. 3256. December.

———.1999b. *Vectors Supercomputers From Japan (Views on Remand)*. Pub. 3166. Investigation No. 731-TA-759 (remand), May, Views of Commissioner Thelma Askey.

———. 2000. *Electroluminescent Flat Panel Displays from Japan*. Investigation No. 7331-TA-469 (Review). Washington, D.C., March 27.

———. 2003a. *Steel Global Safeguards Investigation*. Investigation No. 204-9, September 19, Washington, D.C.

———. 2003b. *Steel Consuming Industries: Competitive Conditions with Respect to Steel Safeguard Measures*, Investigation No. 332-452, September 19, Washington, D.C.

U.S. National Science and Technology Council. 1999. *Computing, Information and Communications: Networked Computing for the 21st Century*. Washington, D.C.: Commission on Physical Sciences, Mathematics, and Applications (CPSMA).

U.S. Securities and Exchange Commission. 2000. *Micron 10K Filing*. Washington, D.C.

Wallison, Peter J. 2003. A Power Shift Nobody Noticed. *Washington Post.* January 12.

Willig, Robert D. 1998. Economic Effects of Antidumping Policy. In Robert Z. Lawrence, ed. *Brookings Trade Forum: Part One, Antidumping.* Washington, D.C.: The Brookings Institution.

Willkie Farr & Gallagher LLP. 2002. Submission to the Department of Commerce Concerning Illegal Subsidies to Hynix. November 5.

World Steel Dynamics. 2001. Financial Dynamics of International Steelmakers. March. http://worldsteeldynamics.com/findyadj.html (accessed November 20, 2002).

World Trade Organization. 1995. The Results of the Uruguay Round of Multilateral Trade Negotiations. *The Legal Texts.* Geneva, Switzerland.

———. 1998. *Communication from the United States to the Working Group on the Interaction between Trade and Competition. WT/WGTCP/W/88.* Geneva, Switzerland. August 28.

———. 2001a. Appellate Body Report: *European Communities—Antidumping Duties on Imports of Cotton-Type Bed Linens from India.* WT/DS141/AB/R. Geneva, Switzerland. March 1.

———. 2001b. Appellate Body Report: *United States—Antidumping Measures on Certain Hot-Rolled Steel Products from Japan.* WT/DS174/AB/R. Geneva, Switzerland. July 24.

———. 2002a. Antidumping Legislation Notifications. *Report of the Committee on Antidumping Practices. G/L/581.* Geneva, Switzerland. October 29.

———. 2002b. Basic Concepts and Principles of the Trade Remedy Rules. *Communication from the United States to the WTO Negotiating Group on Rules. TN/RL/W/27.* Geneva, Switzerland. October 22.

———. 2003a. Semi-Annual Report under Article 16.4 of the Agreement. United States. *G/ADP/N/98/USA.* March 10.

———. 2003b. Semi-Annual Report under Article 16.4 of the Agreement. India. G/ADP/N/98/IND. April 29.

———. 2003c. Semi-Annual Report under Article 16.4 of the Agreement. Brazil. G/ADP/N/98/BRA. February 13.

———. 2003d. Semi-Annual Report under Article 16.4 of the Agreement. Mexico. *G/ADP/N/98/MEX.* April 9.

———. 2003e. Semi-Annual Report under Article 16.4 of the Agreement. European Communities. *G/ADP/N/98/EEC.* March 11.

———. 2003f. Antidumping Initiations/Measures: Reporting Member vs. Affected Country—01/01/95 to 03/12/03. http://www.wto.org/english/ ratop_e/adp_e/ adp_e.htm. Website accessed on July 25, 2003.

Yoon, Chang-ho. 1992. International Competition and Market Penetration: A Model of the Growth Strategy of the Korean Semiconductor Industry. In Gerald K. Helleiner, ed. *Trade Policy, Industrialization, and Development: New Perspectives.* Oxford: Clarendon Press.

About the Author

Claude Barfield is a Resident Scholar at the American Enterprise Institute, where he is Coordinator of Trade Policy Studies and Director of Science and Technology Policy Studies. Mr. Barfield has written extensively and directed numerous research projects on international trade policy. He served as a consultant with the Office of the U.S. Trade Representative during the Reagan administration. He has taught at Yale University, George Washington University, and the University of Munich.

Mr. Barfield's most recent works on trade are *Korea in Asia: Korea's Development, Asian Regionalism and U.S.-Korean Economic Relations* (2003) and *Free Trade, Sovereignty, Democracy: The Future of the World Trade Organization* (2001). His articles on international trade and U.S. competitiveness have appeared in the *Wall Street Journal*, the *New York Times*, and the *Washington Post*.